Bake Sale

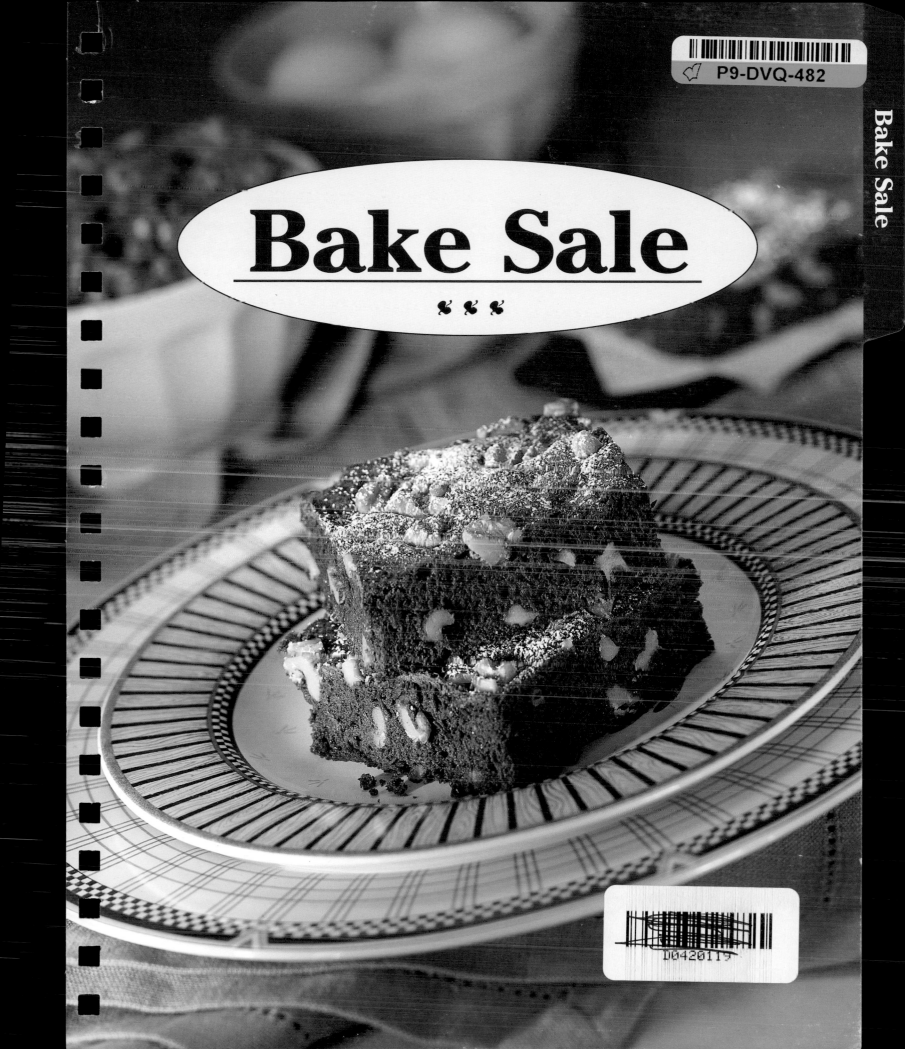

Contents

Bake Sale Basics

There's no doubt about it—bake sales are an American icon. They're not about sophistication or finesse, just simple homemade goodness and tables heaped with every kind of cookie, brownie, pie, cake and muffin imaginable. The best part? Bake sales are happy events: Friends and neighbors baking and sharing their favorite treats, coming together for a good cause.

Bake Sale Savvy

• Bring plenty of price stickers or tags and marking pens.

• Make the math easy (for adding and making change). Price baked goods in increments of 25 cents.

• Increase the bottom line. Offer large bags or containers to encourage customers to buy several items. Auction off whole desserts to raise more money.

• People like to help a worthy cause—be sure the name of your organization is prominently displayed and let customers know how the proceeds will be used.

• Draw attention to the merchandise. Stack brownies and bar cookies high on colorful platters, pile muffins into baskets lined with bright-colored napkins and use decorative boxes or tins to display cookies.

• For single slices of pies and cakes, use plastic deli containers, available at restaurant supply and many party goods stores.

• Include storage directions for any perishable items that should be held in the refrigerator.

• Bake and sell your treats in disposable pans, so you don't have to worry about finding or cleaning your pans after the sale.

• Clearly write the name of the treat on a card that is attached to the item. On the back of the card be sure to list any ingredients that could be a problem for those with food allergies.

• Create a coffee-house atmosphere by setting up tables and chairs so that people can enjoy their treats right away. Also, sell drinks such as coffee, tea and milk.

Dress to Impress

• Wrap stacks of cookies in cellophane or clear bags and tie with curling ribbons.

• For single servings, cut bar cookies to fit into decorative paper or foil baking cups—they will look beautiful and be easier to handle.

• Keep a supply of decorator frosting on hand to offer personalized cakes and cookies throughout the bake sale.

• Cut bar cookies into triangles and diamonds for variety.

• Make cookies stand out by dipping them partially or completely in chocolate.

Simply dip cookies in melted chocolate (milk, dark, white or some of each) and place them on waxed paper until the chocolate has set.

• For any baked goods that are sold whole, such as quick breads, layer cakes or pies, use colored plastic wrap or cellophane and raffia or curling ribbons to package them attractively. Be sure to place cakes on sturdy disposable plastic plates.

Advance Planning

Since bake sales don't always happen when you have time to bake, it's a good idea to plan ahead. Many items can be baked and frozen; some unbaked doughs can also be frozen and later baked up fresh. Not all items freeze well, however, so choose carefully before baking.

• In general, crisp cookies freeze better than soft, moist cookies. Rich, buttery bar cookies are an exception since they freeze extremely well. Thaw frozen cookies and brownies unwrapped at room temperature.

• Meringue-based cookies do not freeze well and chocolate-dipped cookies will discolor if frozen.

• Store cookies with sticky glazes, fragile decorations and icings in single layers between sheets of waxed paper. Bar cookies and brownies can be stored in their own baking pan and covered with aluminum foil or plastic wrap once completely cool.

• Cakes with whipped cream frostings or cream fillings should be stored in the refrigerator. When refrigerating a cake, cover it with plastic wrap to help prevent it from picking up flavors of other foods.

• Cakes with fruit or custard fillings do not freeze well, as they become soggy when thawed.

• Custard, cream and meringue-topped pies should be stored in the refrigerator; they do not freeze well.

• Quick breads should be wrapped well in plastic wrap and stored at room temperature for up to one week, or wrapped in heavy-duty aluminum foil and frozen for up to three months.

• Muffins should be stored in a sealed plastic food storage bag for up to three days, or wrapped in heavy-duty foil and frozen for up to one month.

• To freeze unbaked pies, do not cut steam vents in the top crust. Cover the top with an inverted paper plate for extra protection and package in freezer bags. To bake, do not thaw. Cut slits in the top crust and allow an additional 15 to 20 minutes baking time.

• Baked pies can be cooled and frozen. To serve, let the pie thaw at room temperature for 2 hours, then heat until warm. Pies with cream or custard fillings and meringue toppings are not recommended for freezing.

Great American Cookies

Chocolate-Peanut Butter Checkerboards

½ cup (1 stick) butter or margarine, softened
1 cup sugar
1 egg
1 teaspoon vanilla extract
1 cup plus 3 tablespoons all-purpose flour, divided
½ teaspoon baking soda
¼ cup HERSHEY᳇S Cocoa
½ cup REESE'S® Peanut Butter Chips, melted

1. Beat butter, sugar, egg and vanilla in large bowl until fluffy. Add 1 cup flour and baking soda; beat until blended. Remove ¾ cup batter to small bowl; set aside. Add cocoa and remaining 3 tablespoons flour to remaining batter in large bowl; blend well.

2. Place peanut butter chips in small microwave-safe bowl. Microwave at HIGH (100%) 30 seconds or until melted and smooth when stirred. Immediately add to batter in small bowl, stirring until smooth. Divide chocolate dough into four equal parts. Roll each part between plastic wrap or wax paper into a log 7 inches long and about 1 inch in diameter. Repeat with peanut butter dough. Wrap each roll individually in waxed paper or plastic wrap. Refrigerate several hours until very firm.

3. Heat oven to 350°F. Remove rolls from waxed paper. Place 1 chocolate roll and 1 peanut butter roll side by side on cutting board. Top each roll with another roll of opposite flavor to make checkerboard pattern. Lightly press rolls together; repeat with remaining four rolls. Working with one checkerboard at a time (keep remaining checkerboard covered and refrigerated), cut into ¼-inch slices. Place on ungreased cookie sheet.

4. Bake 8 to 9 minutes or until peanut butter portion is lightly browned. Cool 1 minute; remove from cookie sheet to wire rack. Cool completely. *Makes about 4½ dozen cookies*

Chocolate-Peanut Butter Checkerboards

Lollipop Sugar Cookies

1¼ cups granulated sugar
 1 cup Butter Flavor CRISCO®
   all-vegetable shortening or
   1 Butter Flavor CRISCO® Stick
 2 eggs
 ¼ cup light corn syrup or regular
   pancake syrup
 1 tablespoon vanilla
 3 cups all-purpose flour
 ¾ teaspoon baking powder
 ½ teaspoon baking soda
 ½ teaspoon salt
36 flat ice cream sticks or lollipop sticks
   Any of the following: miniature
   baking chips, raisins, red hots,
   nonpareils, colored sugar or nuts

1. Combine sugar and 1 cup shortening in large bowl. Beat at medium speed of electric mixer until well blended. Add eggs, syrup and vanilla; beat until well blended and fluffy.

2. Combine flour, baking powder, baking soda and salt. Add gradually to creamed mixture at low speed until well blended. Wrap dough in plastic wrap. Refrigerate at least 1 hour.

3. Heat oven to 375°F. Place foil on countertop for cooling cookies.

4. Shape dough into 1½-inch balls. Push ice cream stick into center of each ball. Place balls 3 inches apart on ungreased baking sheet. Flatten balls to ½-inch thickness with bottom of greased and floured glass. Decorate as desired; press decorations gently into dough.*

5. Bake at 375°F for 8 to 10 minutes. *Do not overbake.* Cool on baking sheet 2 minutes. Remove cookies to foil to cool completely.

Makes about 3 dozen cookies

Cookies can also be painted before baking. Mix 1 egg yolk and ¼ teaspoon water. Divide into 3 small cups. Add 2 to 3 drops food color to each. Stir. Use clean water color brushes to paint designs on cookies.

Apple Sauce Gingerbread Cookies

4 cups all-purpose flour
2 teaspoons ground ginger
2 teaspoons ground cinnamon
1 teaspoon baking soda
½ teaspoon salt
¼ teaspoon ground nutmeg
½ cup butter, softened
1 cup sugar
⅓ cup GRANDMA'S® Molasses
1 cup MOTT'S® Natural Apple Sauce
  Decorator Icing (recipe follows)

Heat oven to 350°F. In large bowl, sift together flour, ginger, cinnamon, baking soda, salt and nutmeg; set aside. In bowl of electric mixer, fitted with paddle, beat butter, sugar and molasses until creamy. Alternately blend in dry ingredients and apple sauce. Cover and chill dough for several hours or overnight.

On floured surface, roll dough out to ⅛-inch thickness with lightly floured rolling pin. Cut with floured cookie cutter. Place on greased baking sheet. Bake 12 minutes or until done. Remove from sheet; cool on wire rack. Frost with Decorator Icing as desired. After icing dries, store in airtight container.

Makes 2½ dozen (5½-inch) cookies

Decorator Icing: Mix 2 cups confectioners' sugar and 1 tablespoon water. Add more water, 1 teaspoon at a time, until icing holds its shape and can be piped through decorating tube.

Lollipop Sugar Cookies

White Chip Apricot Oatmeal Cookies

¾ cup (1½ sticks) butter or margarine, softened
½ cup granulated sugar
½ cup packed light brown sugar
1 egg
1 cup all-purpose flour
1 teaspoon baking soda
2½ cups rolled oats
1⅔ cups (10-ounce package) HERSHEY₅S Premier White Chips
¾ cup chopped dried apricots

1. Heat oven to 375°F.

2. Beat butter, granulated sugar and brown sugar in large bowl until fluffy. Add egg; beat well. Add flour and baking soda; beat until well blended. Stir in oats, white chips and apricots. Loosely form rounded teaspoonfuls dough into balls; place on ungreased cookie sheet.

3. Bake 7 to 9 minutes or just until lightly browned; do not overbake. Cool slightly; remove from cookie sheet to wire rack. Cool completely. *Makes about 3½ dozen cookies*

Oatmeal Toffee Cookies

1 cup (2 sticks) butter or margarine, softened
2 eggs
2 cups packed light brown sugar
2 teaspoons vanilla extract
1¾ cups all-purpose flour
1 teaspoon baking soda
1 teaspoon ground cinnamon
½ teaspoon salt
3 cups quick-cooking oats
1¾ cups (10-ounce package) HEATH® BITS 'O BRICKLE Almond Toffee Bits or SKOR® English Toffee Bits
1 cup MOUNDS® Sweetened Coconut Flakes (optional)

1. Heat oven to 375°F. Lightly grease cookie sheet. Beat butter, eggs, brown sugar and vanilla until well blended. Add flour, baking soda, cinnamon and salt; beat until blended.

2. Stir in oats, toffee and coconut, if desired, with spoon. Drop dough by rounded teaspoons about 2 inches apart onto prepared sheet.

3. Bake 8 to 10 minutes or until edges are lightly browned. Cool 1 minute; remove to wire rack. *Makes about 4 dozen cookies*

Chocolate Bursts

6 squares (1 ounce each) semisweet chocolate
½ cup (1 stick) I CAN'T BELIEVE IT'S NOT BUTTER!® Spread
¾ cup sugar
2 eggs
⅓ cup all-purpose flour
¼ cup unsweetened cocoa powder
1½ teaspoons vanilla extract
1 teaspoon baking powder
¼ teaspoon salt
2 cups coarsely chopped pecans or walnuts
1 cup semisweet chocolate chips

Preheat oven to 325°F. Grease baking sheets; set aside.

In medium microwave-safe bowl, heat chocolate squares and I Can't Believe It's Not Butter!® Spread on HIGH (Full Power) 1 to 2 minutes or until chocolate is almost melted. Stir until completely melted.

In large bowl, with electric mixer, beat sugar and eggs until light and ribbony, about 2 minutes. Beat in chocolate mixture, flour, cocoa, vanilla, baking powder and salt, scraping side occasionally, until well blended. Stir in nuts and chocolate chips. Drop dough by rounded tablespoonfuls onto prepared sheets, about 2 inches apart.

Bake 15 minutes or until cookies are just set. On wire rack, let stand 2 minutes; remove from sheets and cool completely.
Makes about 3 dozen cookies

Dreamy Chocolate Chip Cookies

1¼ cups firmly packed brown sugar
¾ Butter Flavor CRISCO® Stick or
    ¾ cup Butter Flavor CRISCO®
    all-vegetable shortening
3 eggs, lightly beaten
2 teaspoons vanilla
1 (4-ounce) package German sweet
    chocolate, melted, cooled
3 cups all-purpose flour
1 teaspoon baking soda
½ teaspoon salt
1 (11½-ounce) package milk chocolate
    chips
1 (10-ounce) package premium
    semisweet chocolate chips
1 cup coarsely chopped macadamia
    nuts

1. Heat oven to 375°F. Place sheets of foil on countertop for cooling cookies.

2. Combine brown sugar, ¾ cup shortening, eggs and vanilla in large bowl. Beat at low speed of electric mixer until blended. Increase speed to high. Beat 2 minutes. Add melted chocolate. Mix until well blended.

3. Combine flour, baking soda and salt. Add gradually to shortening mixture at low speed.

4. Stir in chocolate chips, chocolate pieces and nuts with spoon. Drop by rounded tablespoonfuls 3 inches apart onto ungreased baking sheets.

5. Bake at 375°F for 9 to 11 minutes or until set. *Do not overbake.* Cool 2 minutes on baking sheet. Remove cookies to foil to cool completely.   *Makes about 3 dozen cookies*

Snowballs

½ cup DOMINO® Confectioners 10-X
    Sugar
¼ teaspoon salt
1 cup butter or margarine, softened
1 teaspoon vanilla extract
2¼ cups all-purpose flour
½ cup chopped pecans
    DOMINO® Confectioners 10-X Sugar

In large bowl, combine ½ cup confectioners sugar, salt and butter; mix well. Add extract. Gradually stir in flour. Work nuts into dough. Chill well. Form into 1-inch balls. Place on ungreased cookie sheets. Bake at 400°F for 8 to 10 minutes or until set but not brown. Roll in confectioners sugar immediately. Cool on rack. Roll in sugar again. Store in airtight container.
Makes 5 dozen cookies

Old-Fashioned Molasses Cookies

4 cups sifted all-purpose flour
2 teaspoons ARM & HAMMER®
    Baking Soda
2 teaspoons ground ginger
1 teaspoon ground cinnamon
⅛ teaspoon salt
1½ cups molasses
½ cup butter-flavored shortening
⅓ cup boiling water
    Sugar

In medium bowl, combine flour, Baking Soda, spices and salt. In large bowl, mix molasses, shortening and water. Add dry ingredients to molasses mixture; blend well. Cover; refrigerate until firm, about 2 hours. Roll out dough ¼ inch thick on well-floured surface. Cut out with 3½-inch cookie cutters; sprinkle with sugar. Place 2 inches apart on ungreased cookie sheets. Bake in preheated 375°F oven about 12 minutes. Remove to wire racks to cool.
Makes about 3 dozen cookies

Dreamy Chocolate Chip Cookies

Giant Peanut Butter Cup Cookies

½ cup (1 stick) butter or margarine,
    softened
¾ cup sugar
⅓ cup REESE'S® Creamy or Crunchy
    Peanut Butter
1 egg
½ teaspoon vanilla extract
1¼ cups all-purpose flour
½ teaspoon baking soda
¼ teaspoon salt
16 REESE'S® Peanut Butter Cups
    Miniatures, cut into fourths

1. Heat oven to 350°F.

2. Beat butter, sugar and peanut butter in medium bowl until creamy. Add egg and vanilla; beat well. Stir together flour, baking soda and salt. Add to butter mixture; blend well. Drop dough by level ¼ cup measurements onto ungreased cookie sheets, three cookies per sheet. (Cookies will spread while baking.) Push about seven pieces of peanut butter cup into each cookie, flattening cookie slightly.

3. Bake 15 to 17 minutes or until light golden brown around the edges. Centers will be pale and slightly soft. Cool 1 minute on cookie sheet. Remove to wire rack; cool completely.
Makes 9 cookies

Double Lemon Delights

2¼ cups all-purpose flour
½ teaspoon baking powder
½ teaspoon salt
1 cup (2 sticks) butter, softened
¾ cup granulated sugar
1 egg
2 tablespoons grated lemon peel,
    divided
1 teaspoon vanilla
    Additional sugar
1 cup powdered sugar
4 to 5 teaspoons lemon juice

1. Preheat oven to 375°F.

2. Combine flour, baking powder and salt in small bowl; set aside. Beat butter and granulated sugar in large bowl at medium speed of electric mixer until light and fluffy. Beat in egg, 1 tablespoon lemon peel and vanilla until well blended. Gradually beat in flour mixture on low speed until blended.

3. Drop dough by level ¼ cupfuls onto ungreased cookie sheets, spacing 3 inches apart. Flatten dough until 3 inches in diameter with bottom of glass that has been dipped in additional sugar.

4. Bake 12 to 14 minutes or until cookies are just set and edges are golden brown. Cool on cookie sheets 2 minutes; transfer to wire racks. Cool completely.

5. Combine powdered sugar, lemon juice and remaining 1 tablespoon lemon peel in small bowl; drizzle over cookies. Let stand until icing is set. *Makes about 1 dozen (4-inch) cookies*

Variation: To make smaller cookies, drop 2 tablespoons dough 2 inches apart onto ungreased cookie sheets. Bake 8 to 10 minutes or until cookies are just set and edges are golden brown. Cool on cookie sheets 2 minutes; transfer to wire racks. Cool completely. Continue with Step 5. Makes about 2 dozen cookies.

Chewy Chocolate-Cinnamon Cookies

6 tablespoons butter or margarine,
  softened
⅔ cup packed light brown sugar
3 tablespoons plus ¼ cup granulated
  sugar, divided
¼ cup light corn syrup
1 egg
1 teaspoon vanilla extract
1 teaspoon baking soda
1½ cups all-purpose flour
⅓ cup HERSHEY'S Cocoa
¼ to ½ teaspoon ground cinnamon

1. Heat oven to 350°F. Spray cookie sheet with nonstick cooking spray.

2. Beat butter until creamy. Add brown sugar and 3 tablespoons granulated sugar; beat until blended. Add corn syrup, egg, vanilla and baking soda; beat well.

3. Stir together flour and cocoa; beat into butter mixture. If batter becomes too stiff, use wooden spoon to stir in remaining flour. Cover; refrigerate about 30 minutes, if necessary, until batter is firm enough to shape. Shape dough into 1-inch balls. Combine remaining ¼ cup granulated sugar and cinnamon; roll balls in mixture. Place balls 2 inches apart on prepared cookie sheet.

4. Bake 9 to 10 minutes or until cookies are set and tops are cracked. Cool slightly; remove from cookie sheet to wire rack. Cool completely.
Makes about 40 cookies

Brown Sugar Shortbread

1 cup (2 sticks) I CAN'T BELIEVE
  IT'S NOT BUTTER!® Spread
¾ cup firmly packed light brown sugar
2 cups all-purpose flour
⅓ cup semisweet chocolate chips,
  melted

Preheat oven to 325°F. Grease 9-inch round cake pan; set aside.

In large bowl, with electric mixer, beat I Can't Believe It's Not Butter!® Spread and brown sugar until light and fluffy, about 5 minutes.

Gradually add flour and beat on low until blended. Spread mixture into prepared pan and press into even layer. With knife, score surface into 8 pie-shaped wedges.

Bake 30 minutes or until lightly golden. On wire rack, cool 20 minutes; remove from pan and cool completely. To serve, pour melted chocolate into small plastic storage bag. Snip corner and drizzle chocolate over shortbread. Cut into wedges.
Makes 8 servings

Nutty Footballs

1 cup butter, softened
½ cup sugar
1 egg
½ teaspoon vanilla
2 cups all-purpose flour
¼ cup unsweetened cocoa powder
1 cup finely chopped almonds
  Prepared colored icings (optional)
  White icing

1. Beat butter and sugar in large bowl until creamy. Add egg and vanilla; mix until well blended. Stir together flour and cocoa; gradually add to butter mixture, beating until well blended. Add almonds; beat until well blended. Shape dough into disc. Wrap dough in plastic wrap and refrigerate 30 minutes.

2. Preheat oven to 350°F. Lightly grease cookie sheets. Roll out dough on floured surface to ¼-inch thickness. Cut dough with 2½- to 3-inch football-shaped cookie cutter.* Place 2 inches apart on prepared cookie sheets.

3. Bake 10 to 12 minutes or until set. Cool on cookie sheets 1 to 2 minutes. Remove to wire racks; cool completely. Decorate with colored icings, if desired. Pipe white icing onto footballs to make laces.
Makes 2 dozen cookies

To make footballs without cookie cutter, shape 3 tablespoonfuls of dough into ovals. Place 3 inches apart on prepared cookie sheets. Flatten ovals to ¼-inch thickness; taper ends. Bake as directed.

Nutty Footballs

Choco-Peanut Butter-Brickle Cookies

Prep Time: 15 minutes

1 (14-ounce) can EAGLE BRAND®
    Sweetened Condensed Milk
    (NOT evaporated milk)
1 cup chunky peanut butter
2 eggs
1 teaspoon vanilla extract
1½ cups all-purpose flour
1 teaspoon baking soda
½ teaspoon baking powder
½ teaspoon salt
1 cup (6 ounces) semi-sweet chocolate
    chips
1 cup almond brickle chips

1. Preheat oven to 350°F. In large mixing bowl, beat Eagle Brand, peanut butter, eggs and vanilla until well blended.

2. In medium mixing bowl, combine flour, baking soda, baking powder and salt; add to peanut butter mixture, beating until blended. Stir in chocolate chips and brickle chips. Drop by heaping tablespoonfuls onto lightly greased baking sheets.

3. Bake 12 minutes or until lightly browned. Cool slightly on baking sheets; remove to wire racks to cool.   *Makes 3 dozen cookies*

Super Chocolate Cookies

2 cups all-purpose flour
⅓ cup unsweetened cocoa powder
1 teaspoon baking soda
½ teaspoon salt
½ cup butter, softened
½ cup shortening
1⅓ cups packed brown sugar
2 eggs
2 teaspoons vanilla
1 cup candy-coated chocolate pieces
1 cup raisins
¾ cup salted peanuts, coarsely chopped

1. Preheat oven to 350°F. Combine flour, cocoa, baking soda and salt in medium bowl; set aside.

2. Beat butter, shortening and brown sugar in large bowl of electric mixer at medium speed until light and fluffy. Beat in eggs and vanilla until well blended. Gradually add flour mixture, beating at low speed until blended. Stir in candy pieces, raisins and peanuts.

3. Drop dough by ¼ cupfuls onto ungreased cookie sheets, spacing 3 inches apart. Flatten slightly with fingertips. Bake cookies 13 to 15 minutes or until almost set. Cool 2 minutes on cookie sheets. Transfer to wire racks. Cool completely.   *Makes about 20 (4-inch) cookies*

Chocolate Banana Walnut Drops

½ cup (1 stick) butter or margarine,
    softened
½ cup solid vegetable shortening
1¼ cups firmly packed light brown sugar
1 egg
1 medium banana, mashed (about
    ½ cup)
2¼ cups all-purpose flour
1 teaspoon baking soda
1 teaspoon ground cinnamon
½ teaspoon ground nutmeg
¼ teaspoon salt
2 cups quick-cooking or old-fashioned
    oats, uncooked
1 cup coarsely chopped walnuts
1¾ cups "M&M's"® Chocolate Mini
    Baking Bits

Preheat oven to 350°F. In large bowl cream butter, shortening and sugar until light and fluffy; beat in egg and banana. In medium bowl combine flour, baking soda, cinnamon, nutmeg and salt; blend into creamed mixture. Blend in oats and nuts. Stir in "M&M's"® Chocolate Mini Baking Bits. Drop by tablespoonfuls about 2 inches apart onto ungreased cookie sheets. Bake 8 to 10 minutes just until set. Do not overbake. Cool 1 minute on cookie sheets; cool completely on wire racks. Store in tightly covered container.

Makes about 3 dozen cookies

Chocolate Banana Walnut Drops

Spicy Ginger Molasses Cookies

2 cups all-purpose flour
1½ teaspoons ground ginger
1 teaspoon baking soda
½ teaspoon ground cloves
¼ teaspoon salt
¾ cup (1½ sticks) butter, softened
1 cup sugar
¼ cup molasses
1 egg
   Additional sugar
½ cup yogurt-covered raisins

1. Preheat oven to 375°F. Line cookie sheets with parchment paper.

2. Combine flour, ginger, baking soda, cloves and salt in small bowl; set aside.

3. Beat butter and 1 cup sugar in large bowl of electric mixer at medium speed until light and fluffy. Add molasses and egg; beat until well blended. Gradually beat in flour mixture on low speed just until blended.

4. Drop dough by level ¼ cupfuls onto prepared cookie sheets, spacing 3 inches apart. Flatten dough with bottom of glass dipped in additional sugar until dough is 2 inches in diameter. Press 7 to 8 yogurt-covered raisins into dough of each cookie.

5. Bake 11 to 12 minutes or until cookies are set. Cool cookies 2 minutes on cookie sheets; slide parchment paper and cookies onto countertop. Cool completely.

Makes about 1 dozen (4-inch) cookies

Cranberry Brown Sugar Cookies

Prep Time: 30 minutes
Bake Time: 10 minutes
Cool Time: 30 minutes

2 cups firmly packed DOMINO® Dark
   Brown Sugar
1 cup butter or margarine, softened
2 eggs
½ cup sour cream
3½ cups all-purpose flour
1 teaspoon baking soda
1 teaspoon salt
1 teaspoon ground cinnamon
½ teaspoon ground nutmeg
¼ teaspoon ground cloves
1 cup dried cranberries (5 ounces)
1 cup golden raisins

Heat oven to 400°F. Lightly grease cookie sheets. Beat sugar and butter in large bowl until light and fluffy. Add eggs and sour cream; beat until creamy. Stir together flour, baking soda, salt, cinnamon, nutmeg and cloves in small bowl; gradually add to sugar mixture, beating until well mixed. Stir in cranberries and raisins. Drop by rounded teaspoonfuls onto cookie sheets. Bake 8 to 10 minutes or until lightly browned. Remove from cookie sheets to cooling racks. Cool completely.

Makes about 5 dozen cookies

Note: 1 cup chopped dried cherries may be substituted for 1 cup dried cranberries.

Tip: If cranberries are exceptionally large, chop before adding to cookie dough.

Spicy Ginger Molasses Cookies

Chocolate Cherry Treats

½ cup (1 stick) butter, softened
¾ cup firmly packed light brown sugar
¼ cup granulated sugar
½ cup sour cream
1 egg
1 tablespoon maraschino cherry juice
1 teaspoon vanilla extract
2 cups all-purpose flour
½ teaspoon baking soda
¼ teaspoon salt
1¼ cups "M&M's"® Milk Chocolate Mini
    Baking Bits
½ cup chopped walnuts
⅓ cup well-drained chopped
    maraschino cherries

Preheat oven to 350°F. In large bowl cream butter and sugars until light and fluffy; beat in sour cream, egg, maraschino cherry juice and vanilla. In medium bowl combine flour, baking soda and salt; add to creamed mixture. Stir in "M&M's"® Milk Chocolate Mini Baking Bits, walnuts and maraschino cherries. Drop by heaping tablespoonfuls about 2 inches apart onto ungreased cookie sheets. Bake about 15 minutes. Cool 1 minute on cookie sheets; cool completely on wire racks. Store in tightly covered container. *Makes 3 dozen cookies*

Pinwheel Cookies

½ cup shortening plus additional for
    greasing
⅓ cup plus 1 tablespoon butter, softened
    and divided
2 egg yolks
½ teaspoon vanilla extract
1 package DUNCAN HINES® Moist
    Deluxe® Fudge Marble Cake Mix

1. Combine ½ cup shortening, ⅓ cup butter, egg yolks and vanilla extract in large bowl. Mix at low speed of electric mixer until blended. Set aside cocoa packet from cake mix. Gradually add cake mix. Blend well.

2. Divide dough in half. Add cocoa packet and remaining 1 tablespoon butter to one half of dough. Knead until well blended and chocolate colored.

3. Roll out yellow dough between two pieces of waxed paper into 18×12×⅛-inch rectangle. Repeat with chocolate dough. Remove top pieces of waxed paper from chocolate and yellow doughs. Place yellow dough directly on top of chocolate dough. Remove remaining layers of waxed paper. Roll up jelly-roll fashion, beginning at wide side. Refrigerate 2 hours.

4. Preheat oven to 350°F. Grease baking sheets.

5. Cut dough into ⅛-inch slices. Place sliced dough 1 inch apart on prepared baking sheets. Bake at 350°F for 9 to 11 minutes or until lightly browned. Cool 5 minutes on baking sheets. Remove to cooling racks.
Makes about 3½ dozen cookies

Crunchy Chocolate Chip Cookies

2¼ cups unsifted all-purpose flour
1 teaspoon ARM & HAMMER® Baking
    Soda
1 teaspoon salt
1 cup softened margarine or butter
¾ cup granulated sugar
¾ cup packed brown sugar
1 teaspoon vanilla extract
2 eggs
2 cups (12 ounces) semi-sweet
    chocolate chips
1 cup chopped nuts (peanuts, walnuts
    or pecans)

Preheat oven to 375°F. Sift together flour, Baking Soda and salt in small bowl. Beat margarine, sugars and vanilla in large bowl with electric mixer until creamy. Beat in eggs. Gradually add flour mixture; mix well. Stir in chocolate chips and nuts. Drop by rounded teaspoons onto ungreased cookie sheets. Bake 8 minutes or until lightly browned.
Makes about 8 dozen 2-inch cookies

Pinwheel Cookies

Lone Star Peanut Butter Cutouts

¼ cup smooth peanut butter
¼ cup granulated sugar
3 tablespoons butter or margarine, softened
1¼ cups buttermilk baking mix
2 tablespoons water
½ teaspoon ground cinnamon
⅔ cup dry-roasted peanut halves
½ cup semi-sweet chocolate chips

In a large bowl, stir together peanut butter, sugar and butter or margarine until smooth. Stir in baking mix, water and cinnamon until well blended. Shape dough into a ball. Wrap dough with plastic wrap and chill about 1 hour or until firm. Cut dough in half. Roll each piece ⅛ inch thick on a lightly floured board. Cut dough into shapes with a cookie cutter. Transfer cutouts to ungreased cookie sheets. Press a few roasted peanut halves into the top of each cookie. Bake in a 375°F oven for 8 to 10 minutes, or until golden brown around the edges. With a spatula, transfer cookies to a cooling rack.

Melt chocolate chips in microwave on high power for 2 minutes. Stir until smooth. Drizzle chocolate glaze over each cookie. Refrigerate until glaze is set. Store cookies in an airtight container.   *Makes about 2 dozen cookies*

Favorite recipe from **Texas Peanut Producers Board**

Dark Chocolate Dreams

16 ounces bittersweet chocolate candy bars or bittersweet chocolate chips
¼ cup butter
½ cup all-purpose flour
¾ teaspoon ground cinnamon
½ teaspoon baking powder
¼ teaspoon salt
1½ cups sugar
3 eggs
1 teaspoon vanilla
1 package (12 ounces) white chocolate chips
1 cup chopped pecans, lightly toasted

1. Preheat oven to 350°F. Grease cookie sheets.

2. Coarsely chop chocolate bars; place in microwavable bowl. Add butter. Microwave at HIGH 2 minutes; stir. Microwave 1 to 2 minutes, stirring after 1 minute, or until chocolate is melted. Cool slightly.

3. Combine flour, cinnamon, baking powder and salt in small bowl; set aside.

4. Combine sugar, eggs and vanilla in large bowl of electric mixer. Beat at medium-high speed until very thick and mixture turns pale color, about 6 minutes.

5. Reduce speed to low; slowly beat in chocolate mixture until well blended. Gradually beat in flour mixture until blended. Fold in white chocolate chips and pecans.

6. Drop batter by level ⅓ cupfuls onto prepared cookie sheets, spacing 3 inches apart. Place piece of plastic wrap over dough; flatten dough with fingertips to form 4-inch circles. Remove plastic wrap.

7. Bake 12 minutes or until just firm to the touch and surface begins to crack. *Do not overbake.* Cool cookies 2 minutes on cookie sheets; transfer to wire racks. Cool completely.
        Makes 10 to 12 (5-inch) cookies

Note: Cookies may be baked on ungreased cookie sheets lined with parchment paper. Cool cookies 2 minutes on cookie sheets; slide parchment paper and cookies onto countertop. Cool completely.

Dark Chocolate Dreams

Double Chocolate Oat Cookies

2 cups (12 ounces) semisweet chocolate
    pieces, divided
½ cup (1 stick) margarine or butter,
    softened
½ cup granulated sugar
1 egg
¼ teaspoon vanilla
¾ cup all-purpose flour
¾ cup QUAKER® Oats (quick or old
    fashioned, uncooked)
1 teaspoon baking powder
¼ teaspoon baking soda
¼ teaspoon salt (optional)

Preheat oven to 375°F. Melt 1 cup chocolate
pieces in small saucepan; set aside. Beat
margarine and sugar until fluffy; add melted
chocolate, egg and vanilla. Add combined flour,
oats, baking powder, baking soda and salt; mix
well. Stir in remaining chocolate pieces. Drop
by rounded tablespoonfuls onto *ungreased*
cookie sheets. Bake 8 to 10 minutes. Cool
1 minute on cookie sheets; remove to wire
racks.   *Makes about 3 dozen cookies*

Peanut Butter Crunchies

1 cup granulated sugar
1 cup firmly packed light brown sugar
1 cup JIF® Creamy Peanut Butter
½ Butter Flavor CRISCO® Stick or
    ½ cup Butter Flavor CRISCO®
    all-vegetable shortening
2 eggs
1½ cups all-purpose flour
½ teaspoon baking soda
1 cup peanut butter chips
⅔ cup almond brickle chips

1. Heat oven to 350°F. Place sheets of foil on
countertop for cooling cookies.

2. Combine granulated sugar, brown sugar,
peanut butter and ½ cup shortening in large
bowl. Beat at medium-high speed of electric
mixer until well blended. Beat in eggs.

3. Combine flour and baking soda. Add
gradually to creamed mixture at low speed.
Stir in peanut butter chips and almond brickle

chips with spoon. Shape into 1½-inch balls.
Place 2 inches apart on ungreased baking sheet.
Dip fork in flour; flatten dough slightly in
crisscross pattern.

4. Bake at 350°F for 9 to 11 minutes or until
bottoms are light brown and set. *Do not
overbake*. Cool 5 minutes on baking sheet.
Remove cookies to foil to cool completely.
    Makes about 3 dozen cookies

Hermits

¾ Butter Flavor CRISCO® Stick or
    ¾ cup Butter Flavor CRISCO®
    all-vegetable shortening
1½ cups firmly packed brown sugar
2 tablespoons milk
3 eggs
2½ cups all-purpose flour
1 teaspoon salt
1 teaspoon cinnamon
¾ teaspoon baking soda
¼ teaspoon nutmeg
⅛ teaspoon ground cloves
1 cup raisins
¾ cup chopped walnuts
    Confectioners' sugar

1. Heat oven to 400°F. Place sheets of foil on
countertop for cooling cookies.

2. Combine ¾ cup shortening, sugar and milk
in large bowl. Beat at medium speed of electric
mixer until well blended. Add eggs one at a
time. Beat well after each addition.

3. Combine flour, salt, cinnamon, baking soda,
nutmeg and cloves. Mix into creamed mixture
at low speed just until blended. Stir in raisins
and nuts.

4. Drop level tablespoonfuls of dough 2 inches
apart onto ungreased baking sheet.

5. Bake at 400°F for 7 to 8 minutes, or until
set. *Do not overbake*. Remove cookies to foil to
cool completely. Sift confectioners' sugar over
cooled cookies.   *Makes about 5 dozen cookies*

Peanut Butter Crunchies

Ali's Oatmeal Cookies

1 Butter Flavor CRISCO® Stick or
    1 cup Butter Flavor CRISCO®
    all-vegetable shortening
1 cup granulated sugar
1 cup firmly packed light brown sugar
2 eggs
1 teaspoon vanilla
1½ cups plus 1 tablespoon all-purpose
    flour, divided
1 teaspoon baking soda
¾ teaspoon salt
2½ cups oats (quick or old-fashioned,
    uncooked)
1 cup finely chopped hazelnuts
1 cup finely diced dried apricots
1 cup chopped white chocolate chips

1. Heat oven to 350°F. Place sheets of foil on countertop for cooling cookies.

2. Combine 1 cup shortening, granulated sugar, brown sugar, eggs and vanilla in large bowl. Beat at medium speed of electric mixer until well blended.

3. Combine 1½ cups flour, baking soda and salt. Add gradually to creamed mixture at low speed. Beat until well blended. Stir in oats and nuts with spoon.

4. Toss apricots with remaining 1 tablespoon flour. Stir into dough. Stir in white chocolate chips. Shape into 1½-inch balls. Flatten slightly. Place 2 inches apart on ungreased baking sheet.

5. Bake at 350°F for 11 to 13 minutes or until just beginning to brown around edges and slightly moist in center. *Do not overbake.* Cool 2 minutes on baking sheet. Remove cookies to foil to cool completely.

Makes about 3 dozen cookies

Black & White Hearts

1 cup (2 sticks) butter, softened
¾ cup sugar
1 package (3 ounces) cream cheese,
    softened
1 egg
1½ teaspoons vanilla
3 cups all-purpose flour
1 cup semisweet chocolate chips
2 tablespoons shortening

1. Combine butter, sugar, cream cheese, egg and vanilla in large bowl. Beat at medium speed of electric mixer, scraping bowl often, until light and fluffy. Add flour; beat until well blended. Divide dough in half; wrap each half in waxed paper. Refrigerate 2 hours or until firm.

2. Preheat oven to 375°F. Roll out dough to ⅛-inch thickness on lightly floured surface. Cut dough with lightly floured 2-inch heart-shaped cookie cutter. Place 1 inch apart on ungreased cookie sheets. Bake 7 to 10 minutes or until edges are very lightly browned. Remove immediately to wire racks to cool completely.

3. Melt chocolate chips and shortening in small saucepan over low heat 4 to 6 minutes or until melted. Dip half of each heart into melted chocolate. Refrigerate on cookie sheets or trays lined with waxed paper until chocolate is firm. Store, covered, in refrigerator.

Makes about 3½ dozen cookies

Ali's Oatmeal Cookies

Chocolate Toffee Chip Popcorn Cookies

6 tablespoons margarine or butter, softened
½ cup packed light brown sugar
⅓ cup granulated sugar
2 egg whites
1 teaspoon vanilla extract
1⅓ cups all-purpose flour
1 teaspoon baking soda
2 cups popped NEWMAN'S OWN® Butter Flavored Microwave Popcorn, chopped in food processor
1 cup semisweet chocolate chips
1 (3½-ounce) jar macadamia nuts, chopped (optional)
½ cup uncooked quick-cooking oats
½ cup toffee bits

Preheat oven to 375°F. In large bowl, with mixer at high speed, beat margarine and sugars until light and creamy. Add egg whites and vanilla; beat until smooth. Add flour and baking soda; beat on low speed just until blended. Stir in popcorn, chocolate chips, macadamia nuts, oats and toffee bits. Drop by rounded tablespoonfuls onto *ungreased* cookie sheet. Bake 12 to 15 minutes or until lightly browned. Transfer to wire rack to cool.

Makes about 2½ dozen cookies

Pineapple Oatmeal Crunchies

Prep Time: 20 minutes
Bake Time: 30 minutes per batch

2 cans (8 ounces each) DOLE® Crushed Pineapple
1½ cups margarine
1½ cups packed brown sugar
2 eggs
3 cups all-purpose flour
3 cups old-fashioned rolled oats
1 teaspoon baking powder
1 teaspoon ground cinnamon
½ teaspoon salt
5 bags (1.4 ounces each) chocolate covered toffee nuggets

• Drain crushed pineapple well, reserving ½ cup juice.

• Beat margarine and sugar until light and fluffy. Beat in eggs. Stir in pineapple and reserved juice.

• Combine flour, oats, baking powder, cinnamon and salt. Add to pineapple mixture and mix well. Stir in candy.

• Drop by ¼ cup scoopfuls 1 inch apart onto cookie sheets coated with cooking spray. Flatten slightly. Bake at 375°F 30 minutes.

Makes 24 large cookies

Brownie Turtle Cookies

2 squares (1 ounce each) unsweetened baking chocolate
⅓ cup solid vegetable shortening
1 cup granulated sugar
½ teaspoon vanilla extract
2 eggs
1¼ cups all-purpose flour
½ teaspoon baking powder
½ teaspoon salt
1 cup "M&M's"® Milk Chocolate Mini Baking Bits, divided
1 cup pecan halves
⅓ cup caramel ice cream topping
⅓ cup shredded coconut
⅓ cup finely chopped pecans

Preheat oven to 350°F. Lightly grease cookie sheets; set aside. Heat chocolate and shortening in 2-quart saucepan over low heat, stirring constantly until melted; remove from heat. Mix in sugar, vanilla and eggs. Blend in flour, baking powder and salt. Stir in ⅔ cup "M&M's"® Milk Chocolate Mini Baking Bits. For each cookie, arrange 3 pecan halves, with ends almost touching at center, on prepared cookie sheets. Drop dough by rounded teaspoonfuls onto center of each group of pecans; mound the dough slightly. Bake 8 to 10 minutes just until set. *Do not overbake.* Cool completely on wire racks. In small bowl combine ice cream topping, coconut and chopped nuts; top each cookie with about 1½ teaspoons mixture. Press remaining ⅓ cup "M&M's"® Milk Chocolate Mini Baking Bits into topping.

Makes about 2½ dozen cookies

Brownie Turtle Cookies

Chocolate Peanut Butter Chip Cookies

Prep Time: 15 minutes
Bake Time: 6 to 8 minutes

8 (1-ounce) squares semi-sweet
    chocolate
3 tablespoons butter or margarine
1 (14-ounce) can EAGLE BRAND®
    Sweetened Condensed Milk
    (NOT evaporated milk)
2 cups biscuit baking mix
1 egg
1 teaspoon vanilla extract
1 cup (6 ounces) peanut butter-flavored
    chips

1. Preheat oven to 350°F. In large saucepan over low heat, melt chocolate and butter with Eagle Brand; remove from heat. Add baking mix, egg and vanilla; with mixer, beat until smooth and well blended.

2. Let mixture cool to room temperature. Stir in peanut butter chips. Shape into 1¼-inch balls. Place 2 inches apart on ungreased baking sheets. Bake 6 to 8 minutes or until tops are lightly crusty. Cool. Store tightly covered at room temperature.

Makes about 4 dozen cookies

White Chocolate Chunk & Macadamia Nut Brownie Cookies

1½ cups firmly packed light brown sugar
⅔ CRISCO® Stick or ⅔ cup CRISCO®
    all-vegetable shortening
1 tablespoon water
1 teaspoon vanilla
2 eggs
1½ cups all-purpose flour
⅓ cup unsweetened cocoa powder
½ teaspoon salt
¼ teaspoon baking soda
1 cup white chocolate chunks or chips
1 cup coarsely chopped macadamia
    nuts

1. Heat oven to 375°F. Place sheets of foil on countertop for cooling cookies.

2. Place brown sugar, ⅔ cup shortening, water and vanilla in large bowl. Beat at medium speed of electric mixer until well blended. Add eggs; beat well.

3. Combine flour, cocoa, salt and baking soda. Add to shortening mixture; beat at low speed just until blended. Stir in white chocolate chunks and macadamia nuts.

4. Drop dough by rounded measuring tablespoonfuls 2 inches apart onto ungreased baking sheet.

5. Bake one baking sheet at a time at 375°F for 7 to 9 minutes or until cookies are set. *Do not overbake.* Cool 2 minutes on baking sheet. Remove cookies to foil to cool completely.

Makes about 3 dozen cookies

Chocolate Peanut Butter Chip Cookies

Best-Selling Bars & Brownies

Toffee-Top Cheesecake Bars

Prep Time: 20 minutes
Bake Time: 40 minutes
Cool Time: 15 minutes

- 1¼ cups all-purpose flour
- 1 cup powdered sugar
- ½ cup unsweetened cocoa
- ¼ teaspoon baking soda
- ¾ cup (1½ sticks) butter or margarine
- 1 (8-ounce) package cream cheese, softened
- 1 (14-ounce) can EAGLE BRAND® Sweetened Condensed Milk (NOT evaporated milk)
- 2 eggs
- 1 teaspoon vanilla extract
- 1½ cups (8-ounce package) English toffee bits, divided

1. Preheat oven to 350°F. In medium mixing bowl, combine flour, powdered sugar, cocoa and baking soda; cut in butter until mixture is crumbly. Press firmly on bottom of ungreased 13×9-inch baking pan. Bake 15 minutes.

2. In large mixing bowl, beat cream cheese until fluffy. Add Eagle Brand, eggs and vanilla; beat until smooth. Stir in 1 cup English toffee bits. Pour mixture over hot crust. Bake 25 minutes or until set and edges just begin to brown.

3. Remove from oven. Cool 15 minutes. Sprinkle remaining ½ cup English toffee bits evenly over top. Cool completely. Refrigerate several hours or until cold. Store leftovers covered in refrigerator.

Makes about 36 bars

Toffee-Top Cheesecake Bars

Hershey's Best Brownies

1 cup (2 sticks) butter or margarine
2 cups sugar
2 teaspoons vanilla extract
4 eggs
¾ cup HERSHEY₃S Cocoa or
    HERSHEY₃S Dutch Processed
    Cocoa
1 cup all-purpose flour
½ teaspoon baking powder
¼ teaspoon salt
1 cup chopped nuts (optional)

1. Heat oven to 350°F. Grease 13×9×2-inch baking pan.

2. Place butter in large microwave-safe bowl. Microwave at HIGH (100%) 2 to 2½ minutes or until melted. Stir in sugar and vanilla. Add eggs, one at a time, beating well with spoon after each addition. Add cocoa; beat until well blended. Add flour, baking powder and salt; beat well. Stir in nuts, if desired. Pour batter into prepared pan.

3. Bake 30 to 35 minutes or until brownies begin to pull away from sides of pan. Cool completely in pan on wire rack. Cut into bars.

Makes about 36 brownies

Double Decker Bars

Prep Time: 20 minutes
Bake Time: 35 minutes

3 ripe DOLE® Bananas, divided
½ cup margarine
1 cup granulated sugar
1 cup packed brown sugar
2 eggs
¼ cup plus 3 tablespoons peanut butter,
    divided
1 teaspoon vanilla extract
2 cups all-purpose flour
2 teaspoons baking powder
¼ teaspoon salt
2 tablespoons milk
2½ cups powdered sugar

• Blend 1 banana in blender. Beat margarine, granulated sugar and brown sugar in large

bowl. Beat in puréed banana, eggs, 3 tablespoons peanut butter and vanilla.

• Combine flour, baking powder and salt in medium bowl. Gradually beat dry ingredients into banana mixture.

• Spread half of batter in greased 13×9-inch baking pan. Finely chop 1 banana; sprinkle over batter in pan. Cover with remaining batter.

• Bake at 350°F, 30 to 35 minutes. Cool completely.

Peanut Butter Frosting
• Blend remaining banana in blender. Combine banana, remaining peanut butter and milk. Slowly beat in powdered sugar until thick and smooth. Frost bars. *Makes 24 bars*

Apricot Honey Oat Bar Cookies

1½ cups old-fashioned rolled oats,
    uncooked
½ cup finely chopped dried apricots
½ cup honey
¼ cup nonfat plain yogurt
2 egg whites
3 tablespoons butter or margarine,
    melted
2 tablespoons wheat germ
2 tablespoons all-purpose flour
½ teaspoon ground cinnamon
½ teaspoon vanilla
¼ teaspoon salt

Spray 8-inch square baking pan with nonstick cooking spray. Combine all ingredients in large bowl; mix well. Spread mixture evenly into prepared pan. Bake at 325°F about 25 minutes or until center is firm and edges are lightly browned. Cool and cut into 2-inch squares.

Makes 8 servings

Favorite recipe from **National Honey Board**

Hershey's Best Brownies

Fabulous Fruit Bars

1½ cups all-purpose flour, divided
1½ cups sugar, divided
½ cup MOTT'S® Apple Sauce, divided
½ teaspoon baking powder
2 tablespoons margarine
½ cup chopped peeled apple
½ cup chopped dried apricots
½ cup chopped cranberries
1 whole egg
1 egg white
1 teaspoon lemon juice
½ teaspoon vanilla extract
1 teaspoon ground cinnamon

1. Preheat oven to 350°F. Spray 13×9-inch baking pan with nonstick cooking spray.

2. In medium bowl, combine 1¼ cups flour, ½ cup sugar, ⅓ cup apple sauce and baking powder. Cut in margarine with pastry blender or fork until mixture resembles coarse crumbs.

3. In large bowl, combine apple, apricots, cranberries, remaining apple sauce, whole egg, egg white, lemon juice and vanilla.

4. In small bowl, combine remaining 1 cup sugar, ¼ cup flour and cinnamon. Add to fruit mixture, stirring just until mixed.

5. Press half of crumb mixture evenly into bottom of prepared pan. Top with fruit mixture. Sprinkle with remaining crumb mixture.

6. Bake 40 minutes or until lightly browned. Broil, 4 inches from heat, 1 to 2 minutes or until golden brown. Cool on wire rack 15 minutes; cut into 16 bars.

Makes 16 servings

Emily's Dream Bars

½ Butter Flavor CRISCO® Stick or ½ cup Butter Flavor CRISCO® all-vegetable shortening plus additional for greasing
1 cup JIF® Crunchy Peanut Butter
½ cup firmly packed brown sugar
½ cup light corn syrup
1 egg
1 teaspoon vanilla
1 cup all-purpose flour
½ teaspoon baking powder
¼ cup milk
2 cups 100% natural oats, honey and raisins cereal
1 package (12 ounces) miniature semisweet chocolate chips (2 cups), divided
1 cup almond brickle chips
1 cup milk chocolate covered peanuts
1 package (2 ounces) nut topping (⅓ cup)

1. Heat oven to 350°F. Grease 13×9×2-inch pan with shortening. Place wire rack on countertop for cooling bars.

2. Combine ½ cup shortening, peanut butter, brown sugar and corn syrup in large bowl. Beat at medium speed of electric mixer until creamy. Add egg and vanilla. Beat well.

3. Combine flour and baking powder. Add alternately with milk to creamed mixture at medium speed. Stir in cereal, 1 cup chocolate chips, almond brickle chips and chocolate covered nuts with spoon. Spread evenly in prepared pan.

4. Bake at 350°F for 20 to 26 minutes or until golden brown and toothpick inserted in center comes out clean. *Do not overbake.* Sprinkle remaining 1 cup chocolate chips over top immediately after removing from oven. Remove pan to wire rack. Let stand about 3 minutes or until chips become shiny and soft. Spread over top. Sprinkle with nut topping. Cool completely. Cut into 2×1-inch bars.

Makes 4½ dozen bars

Fabulous Fruit Bars

Candy Bar Bars

Prep Time: 20 minutes
Bake Time: 40 minutes

¾ cup (1½ sticks) butter or margarine, softened
¼ cup peanut butter
1 cup firmly packed light brown sugar
1 teaspoon baking soda
2 cups quick-cooking oats
1½ cups all-purpose flour
1 egg
1 (14-ounce) can EAGLE BRAND® Sweetened Condensed Milk (NOT evaporated milk)
4 cups chopped candy bars (such as chocolate-covered caramel-topped nougat bars with peanuts, chocolate-covered crisp wafers, chocolate-covered caramel-topped cookie bars, or chocolate-covered peanut butter cups)

1. Preheat oven to 350°F. In large mixing bowl, combine butter and peanut butter. Add brown sugar and baking soda; beat well. Stir in oats and flour. Reserve 1¾ cups crumb mixture.

2. Stir egg into remaining crumb mixture; press firmly on bottom of ungreased 15×10×1-inch baking pan. Bake 15 minutes.

3. Pour Eagle Brand evenly over baked crust. Stir together reserved crumb mixture and candy bar pieces; sprinkle evenly over top. Bake 25 minutes or until golden. Cool. Cut into bars. Store covered at room temperature.
Makes 4 dozen bars

Easy Turtle Squares

1 package (about 18 ounces) chocolate cake mix
½ cup butter, melted
¼ cup milk
1 cup (6-ounce package) semisweet chocolate chips
1 cup chopped pecans, divided
1 jar (12 ounces) caramel ice cream topping

1. Preheat oven to 350°F. Spray 13×9-inch pan with nonstick cooking spray.

2. Combine cake mix, butter and milk in large bowl. Press half of mixture into prepared pan.

3. Bake 7 to 8 minutes or until batter begins to form crust. Carefully remove from oven. Sprinkle chocolate chips and ½ cup pecans over partially baked crust. Drizzle caramel topping over chips and pecans. Drop spoonfuls of remaining cake batter over caramel mixture; sprinkle with remaining ½ cup pecans.

4. Return to oven; bake 18 to 20 minutes longer or until top of cake layer springs back when lightly touched. (Caramel center will be soft.) Cool completely on wire rack. Cut into squares. *Makes 24 bar cookies*

Marbled Peanut Butter Brownies

½ cup butter, softened
¼ cup peanut butter
1 cup packed light brown sugar
½ cup granulated sugar
3 eggs
1 teaspoon vanilla
2 cups all-purpose flour
2 teaspoons baking powder
⅛ teaspoon salt
1 cup chocolate syrup
½ cup coarsely chopped salted mixed nuts

Preheat oven to 350°F. Lightly grease 13×9-inch pan. Beat butter and peanut butter in large bowl until blended; stir in sugars. Beat in eggs, one at a time, until well blended. Blend in vanilla. Combine flour, baking powder and salt in small bowl. Stir into butter mixture. Spread half of batter evenly in prepared pan. Spread syrup over top. Spoon remaining batter over syrup. Swirl with knife or spatula to create marbled effect. Sprinkle with chopped nuts. Bake 35 to 40 minutes or until lightly browned. Cool in pan on wire rack. Cut into 2-inch squares. *Makes about 2 dozen brownies*

Easy Turtle Squares

Caramel Apple Bars

Crust

¾ Butter Flavor CRISCO® Stick or
¾ cup Butter Flavor CRISCO®
all-vegetable shortening plus
additional for greasing
1 cup firmly packed light brown sugar
1 egg
1½ cups all-purpose flour
½ teaspoon salt
½ teaspoon baking soda
1¾ cups quick oats (not instant or
old-fashioned), uncooked

Filling

3 to 4 Granny Smith or Golden
Delicious apples, peeled and cut
into ½-inch dice (about 4 cups)
2 tablespoons all-purpose flour
1 teaspoon lemon juice
1 bag (14 ounces) caramel candy,
unwrapped

1. Heat oven to 350°F. Grease 13×9×2-inch baking pan with shortening.

2. For crust, combine ¾ cup shortening and brown sugar in large bowl. Beat at medium speed of electric mixer until well blended. Add egg to creamed mixture. Beat until well blended.

3. Mix 1½ cups flour, salt and baking soda. Add to creamed mixture gradually. Stir in oats until blended. Reserve 1¼ cups of mixture for topping. Press remaining mixture into prepared pan.

4. Bake at 350°F for 10 minutes.

5. For filling, toss apples with 2 tablespoons flour and lemon juice. Distribute apple mixture evenly over partially baked crust. Press lightly.

6. Place caramels in microwave-safe bowl. Microwave at HIGH (100%) for 1 minute. Stir. Repeat until caramels are melted. Drizzle melted caramel evenly over apples. Crumble reserved topping evenly over caramel.

7. Bake at 350°F for 30 to 40 minutes, or until apples are tender and top is golden brown. *Do not overbake.* Loosen caramel from sides of pan with knife. Cool completely. Cut into 1½-inch bars. Cover tightly with plastic wrap to store.

Makes about 4 dozen bars

Chocolate Nut Bars

Prep Time: 10 minutes
Bake Time: 33 to 38 minutes

1¾ cups graham cracker crumbs
½ cup (1 stick) butter or margarine,
melted
1 (14-ounce) can EAGLE BRAND®
Sweetened Condensed Milk
(NOT evaporated milk)
2 cups (12 ounces) semi-sweet
chocolate chips, divided
1 teaspoon vanilla extract
1 cup chopped nuts

1. Preheat oven to 375°F. In medium mixing bowl, combine crumbs and butter; press firmly on bottom of ungreased 13×9-inch baking pan. Bake 8 minutes. Reduce oven temperature to 350°F.

2. In small saucepan, melt Eagle Brand with 1 cup chips and vanilla. Spread chocolate mixture over prepared crust. Top with remaining 1 cup chips and nuts; press down firmly.

3. Bake 25 to 30 minutes. Cool. Chill, if desired. Cut into bars. Store loosely covered at room temperature. *Makes 24 to 36 bars*

Chocolate Nut Bars

Cranberry Cheese Bars

2 cups all-purpose flour
1½ cups quick-cooking or old-fashioned oats, uncooked
¾ cup plus 1 tablespoon firmly packed light brown sugar, divided
1 cup (2 sticks) butter or margarine, softened
1¾ cups "M&M's"® Chocolate Mini Baking Bits, divided
1 (8-ounce) package cream cheese
1 (14-ounce) can sweetened condensed milk
¼ cup lemon juice
1 teaspoon vanilla extract
2 tablespoons cornstarch
1 (16-ounce) can whole berry cranberry sauce

Preheat oven to 350°F. Lightly grease 13×9×2-inch baking pan; set aside. In large bowl combine flour, oats, ¾ cup sugar and butter; mix until crumbly. Reserve 1½ cups crumb mixture for topping. Stir ½ cup "M&M's"® Chocolate Mini Baking Bits into remaining crumb mixture; press into prepared pan. Bake 15 minutes. Cool completely. In large bowl beat cream cheese until light and fluffy; gradually mix in condensed milk, lemon juice and vanilla until smooth. Pour evenly over crust. In small bowl combine remaining 1 tablespoon sugar, cornstarch and cranberry sauce. Spoon over cream cheese mixture. Stir remaining 1¼ cups "M&M's"® Chocolate Mini Baking Bits into reserved crumb mixture. Sprinkle over cranberry mixture. Bake 40 minutes. Cool at room temperature; refrigerate before cutting. Store in refrigerator in tightly covered container. *Makes 32 bars*

Mississippi Mud Brownies

1 (21-ounce) package DUNCAN HINES® Family-Style Chewy Fudge Brownie Mix
2 eggs
⅓ cup water
⅓ cup vegetable oil plus additional for greasing
1 jar (7 ounces) marshmallow creme
1 container DUNCAN HINES® Milk Chocolate Frosting, melted

1. Preheat oven to 350°F. Grease bottom only of 13×9-inch pan.

2. Combine brownie mix, eggs, water and oil in large bowl. Stir with spoon until well blended, about 50 strokes. Spread in pan. Bake at 350°F for 25 to 28 minutes or until set.

3. Spread marshmallow creme gently over hot brownies. Pour 1¼ cups melted milk chocolate frosting over marshmallow creme. Swirl with knife to marble. Cool completely. Cut into bars.
Makes 20 to 24 brownies

Note: Store leftover melted frosting in original container. Refrigerate.

Buttery Black Raspberry Bars

1 cup butter or margarine
1 cup sugar
2 egg yolks
2 cups all-purpose flour
1 cup chopped walnuts
½ cup SMUCKER'S® Seedless Black Raspberry Jam

Beat butter until soft and creamy. Gradually add sugar, beating until mixture is light and fluffy. Add egg yolks; blend well. Gradually add flour; mix thoroughly. Fold in walnuts.

Spoon half of batter into greased 8-inch square pan; spread evenly. Top with jam; cover with remaining batter.

Bake at 325°F for 1 hour or until lightly browned. Cool and cut into 2×1-inch bars.
Makes 32 bars

Cranberry Cheese Bars

Rocky Road Bars

2 cups (12-ounce package) NESTLÉ®
    TOLL HOUSE® Semi-Sweet
    Chocolate Morsels, *divided*
1½ cups all-purpose flour
1½ teaspoons baking powder
1 cup granulated sugar
6 tablespoons (¾ stick) butter or
    margarine, softened
1½ teaspoons vanilla extract
2 eggs
2 cups miniature marshmallows
1½ cups coarsely chopped walnuts

PREHEAT oven to 375°F. Grease 13×9-inch baking pan.

MICROWAVE *1 cup* morsels in medium, uncovered, microwave-safe bowl on HIGH (100%) power for 1 minute. STIR. Morsels may retain some of their original shape. If necessary, microwave at additional 10- to 15-second intervals, stirring just until morsels are melted. Cool to room temperature. Combine flour and baking powder in small bowl.

BEAT sugar, butter and vanilla in large mixer bowl until crumbly. Beat in eggs. Add melted chocolate; beat until smooth. Gradually beat in flour mixture. Spread batter into prepared baking pan.

BAKE for 16 to 20 minutes or until wooden pick inserted in center comes out slightly sticky.

REMOVE from oven; sprinkle immediately with marshmallows, nuts and *remaining* morsels. Return to oven for 2 minutes or just until marshmallows begin to melt. Cool in pan on wire rack for 20 to 30 minutes. Cut into bars with wet knife. Serve warm.

Makes 2½ dozen bars

Cheesecake-Topped Brownies

Prep Time: 20 minutes
Bake Time: 40 to 45 minutes

1 (21.5- or 23.6-ounce) package fudge
    brownie mix
1 (8-ounce) package cream cheese,
    softened
2 tablespoons butter or margarine,
    softened
1 tablespoon cornstarch
1 (14-ounce) can EAGLE BRAND®
    Sweetened Condensed Milk
    (NOT evaporated milk)
1 egg
2 teaspoons vanilla extract
    Ready-to-spread chocolate frosting, if
    desired
    Orange peel, if desired

1. Preheat oven to 350°F. Prepare brownie mix as package directs. Spread into well-greased 13×9-inch baking pan.

2. In large mixing bowl, beat cream cheese, butter and cornstarch until fluffy.

3. Gradually beat in Eagle Brand. Add egg and vanilla; beat until smooth. Pour cheesecake mixture evenly over brownie batter.

4. Bake 40 to 45 minutes or until top is lightly browned. Cool. Spread with frosting or sprinkle with orange peel, if desired. Cut into bars. Store covered in refrigerator.

Makes 3 to 3½ dozen brownies

Cheesecake-Topped Brownies

Brownie Caramel Pecan Bars

½ cup sugar
2 tablespoons butter or margarine
2 tablespoons water
2 cups (12-ounce package)
  HERSHEY₅S Semi-Sweet
  Chocolate Chips, divided
2 eggs
1 teaspoon vanilla extract
⅔ cup all-purpose flour
¼ teaspoon baking soda
¼ teaspoon salt
  Classic Caramel Topping (recipe
  follows)
1 cup pecan pieces

1. Heat oven to 350°F. Line 9-inch square baking pan with foil, extending foil over edges of pan. Grease and flour foil.

2. Combine sugar, butter and water in medium saucepan. Cook over low heat, stirring constantly, until mixture boils. Remove from heat. Immediately add 1 cup chocolate chips; stir until melted. Beat in eggs and vanilla until well blended. Stir together flour, baking soda and salt; stir into chocolate mixture. Spread batter into prepared pan.

3. Bake 15 to 20 minutes or until brownies begin to pull away from sides of pan. Meanwhile, prepare Classic Caramel Topping. Remove brownies from oven; immediately and carefully spread with prepared topping. Sprinkle remaining 1 cup chips and pecans over topping. Cool completely in pan on wire rack, being careful not to disturb chips while soft. Lift out of pan. Cut into bars.

Makes about 16 bars

Classic Caramel Topping: Remove wrappers from 25 HERSHEY₅S Classic Caramels. Combine ¼ cup (½ stick) butter or margarine, caramels and 2 tablespoons milk in medium microwave-safe bowl. Microwave at HIGH (100%) 1 minute; stir. Microwave an additional 1 to 2 minutes, stirring every 30 seconds, or until caramels are melted and mixture is smooth when stirred. Use immediately.

Raspberry Crisp Bars

Crust
  ½ Butter Flavor CRISCO® Stick or
  ½ cup Butter Flavor CRISCO®
    all-vegetable shortening
  ⅓ cup confectioners' sugar
  1 cup all-purpose flour

Topping
  ½ cup all-purpose flour
  3 tablespoons firmly packed light
    brown sugar
  ¼ teaspoon baking powder
  ¼ teaspoon ground cinnamon
  4 tablespoons Butter Flavor CRISCO®
    all-vegetable shortening
  1 egg yolk
  ½ teaspoon vanilla
  ¾ cup SMUCKER'S® Raspberry
    Preserves or any flavor

1. Heat oven to 350°F.

2. For crust, combine ½ cup shortening and confectioners' sugar in large bowl. Beat at medium speed with electric mixer until well blended. Stir in 1 cup flour until mixture is just crumbly. Press into bottom of ungreased 8-inch square baking pan. Bake at 350°F for 10 to 12 minutes or until crust is set but not browned. Remove from oven and place on cooling rack.

3. For topping, combine ½ cup flour, brown sugar, baking powder and cinnamon in medium bowl; mix well. Cut in shortening with fork until mixture forms even crumbs. Add egg yolk and vanilla; mix well.

4. Spread preserves evenly over crust. Sprinkle topping evenly over preserves. Bake at 350°F for 30 minutes or until topping is golden. Place on cooling rack and allow to cool completely. Cut into bars.

Makes 1 dozen bars

Brownie Caramel Pecan Bars

Yellow's Nuts for Nutty Squares

1 cup (2 sticks) plus 2 tablespoons
    butter, softened and divided
½ cup powdered sugar
2¼ cups all-purpose flour
¼ teaspoon salt
¾ cup granulated sugar
½ cup light corn syrup
2 eggs, beaten
½ teaspoon vanilla extract
2 cups coarsely chopped mixed nuts
1 cup "M&M's"® Semi-Sweet
    Chocolate Mini Baking Bits

Preheat oven to 325°F. Lightly grease 13×9-inch baking pan; set aside. In large bowl beat 1 cup (2 sticks) butter and powdered sugar; gradually add flour and salt until well blended. Press dough evenly onto bottom and ½ inch up sides of prepared pan. Bake 25 to 30 minutes or until very light golden brown. In small saucepan melt remaining 2 tablespoons butter; let cool slightly. In large bowl combine melted butter, granulated sugar, corn syrup, eggs and vanilla. Pour filling over partially baked crust; sprinkle with nuts and "M&M's"® Semi-Sweet Chocolate Mini Baking Bits. Return to oven; bake 30 to 35 minutes or until filling is set. Remove pan to wire rack; cool completely. Cut into bars. Store in tightly covered container. *Makes 2 dozen bars*

Nuggets o' Gold Brownies

3 ounces unsweetened baking chocolate
¼ cup WESSON® Vegetable Oil
2 eggs
1 cup sugar
1 teaspoon vanilla extract
¼ teaspoon salt
½ cup all-purpose flour
1 (3.8-ounce) BUTTERFINGER®
    Candy Bar, coarsely chopped

In microwave-safe measuring cup, heat chocolate 2 minutes on HIGH in microwave oven. Stir and continue heating in 30-second intervals until chocolate is completely melted. Stir in oil and set aside to cool. In mixing bowl, beat eggs until foamy. Whisk in sugar, then add vanilla and salt. Stir in chocolate mixture, then mix in flour until all ingredients are moistened. Gently fold in candy. Pour batter into greased 9-inch baking pan and bake at 350°F for 25 to 30 minutes or until edges begin to pull away from sides of pan. Cool before cutting.
Makes 20 brownies

Double Decadence Chocolate Chip Brownies

1 cup granulated sugar
1 stick plus 3 tablespoons margarine
    or butter, softened
2 eggs
1 teaspoon vanilla
2 cups (12 ounces) semisweet chocolate
    pieces, divided
1¼ cups all-purpose flour
1 cup QUAKER® Oats (quick or old
    fashioned, uncooked)
1 teaspoon baking powder
½ cup chopped nuts (optional)
    Powdered sugar

Heat oven to 350°F. Lightly grease 13×9-inch baking pan. Beat sugar, margarine, eggs and vanilla until smooth. Add 1 cup chocolate pieces, melted;* mix well. Add flour, oats, baking powder, remaining 1 cup chocolate pieces and nuts, mixing well. Spread into prepared pan. Bake 25 to 30 minutes or until brownies just begin to pull away from sides of pan. Cool completely. Sprinkle with powdered sugar, if desired. Cut into bars.
Makes 2 dozen brownies

To melt 1 cup chocolate pieces: Microwave at HIGH 1 to 2 minutes, stirring every 30 seconds until smooth. Or, heat in heavy saucepan over low heat, stirring until smooth.

Decadent Blonde Brownies

1½ cups all-purpose flour
1 teaspoon baking powder
½ teaspoon salt
¾ cup granulated sugar
¾ cup packed light brown sugar
½ cup (1 stick) butter, softened
2 eggs
2 teaspoons vanilla
1 package (10 ounces) semisweet chocolate chunks*
1 jar (3½ ounces) macadamia nuts, coarsely chopped, to measure ¾ cup

*If chocolate chunks are not available, cut 1 (10-ounce) thick chocolate candy bar into ¼-inch pieces to measure 1½ cups.

1. Preheat oven to 350°F. Grease 13×9-inch baking pan. Combine flour, baking powder and salt in small bowl; set aside.

2. Beat granulated sugar, brown sugar and butter in large bowl with electric mixer at medium speed until light and fluffy. Beat in eggs and vanilla. Add flour mixture. Beat at low speed until well blended. Stir in chocolate chunks and macadamia nuts. Spread batter evenly in prepared pan. Bake 25 to 30 minutes or until golden brown. Remove pan to wire rack; cool completely. Cut into 3¼×1½-inch bars.   *Makes 2 dozen brownies*

Magic Cookie Bars

Prep Time: 10 minutes
Bake Time: 25 minutes

½ cup (1 stick) butter or margarine
1½ cups graham cracker crumbs
1 (14-ounce) can EAGLE BRAND® Sweetened Condensed Milk (NOT evaporated milk)
2 cups (12 ounces) semi-sweet chocolate chips
1⅓ cups flaked coconut
1 cup chopped nuts

1. Preheat oven to 350°F (325°F for glass dish). In 13×9-inch baking pan, melt butter in oven.

2. Sprinkle crumbs over butter; pour Eagle Brand evenly over crumbs. Layer evenly with remaining ingredients; press down firmly.

3. Bake 25 minutes or until lightly browned. Cool. Chill, if desired. Cut into bars. Store loosely covered at room temperature.
          Makes 2 to 3 dozen bars

7-Layer Magic Cookie Bars: Substitute 1 cup (6 ounces) butterscotch-flavored chips for 1 cup semi-sweet chocolate chips. (Peanut butter-flavored chips or white chocolate chips can be substituted for butterscotch-flavored chips.)

Magic Peanut Cookie Bars: Substitute 2 cups (about ¾ pound) chocolate-covered peanuts for semi-sweet chocolate chips and chopped nuts.

Magic Rainbow Cookie Bars: Substitute 2 cups plain candy-coated chocolate pieces for semi-sweet chocolate chips.

Chewy Butterscotch Brownies

2½ cups all-purpose flour
1 teaspoon baking powder
½ teaspoon salt
1 cup (2 sticks) butter or margarine, softened
1¾ cups packed brown sugar
1 tablespoon vanilla extract
2 eggs
1⅔ cups (11-ounce package) NESTLÉ® TOLL HOUSE® Butterscotch Flavored Morsels, *divided*
1 cup chopped nuts

PREHEAT oven to 350°F.

COMBINE flour, baking powder and salt in medium bowl. Beat butter, sugar and vanilla extract in large mixer bowl until creamy. Beat in eggs. Gradually beat in flour mixture. Stir in *1 cup* morsels and nuts. Spread into ungreased 13×9-inch baking pan. Sprinkle with *remaining* morsels.

BAKE for 30 to 40 minutes or until wooden pick inserted in center comes out clean. Cool in pan on wire rack. Cut into bars.
          Makes about 4 dozen brownies

Magic Cookie Bars

Triple Chocolate Brownies

3 squares (1 ounce each) unsweetened
    chocolate, coarsely chopped
2 squares (1 ounce each) semisweet
    chocolate, coarsely chopped
½ cup (1 stick) butter
1 cup all-purpose flour
½ teaspoon salt
¼ teaspoon baking powder
1½ cups sugar
3 eggs
1 teaspoon vanilla
¼ cup sour cream
½ cup milk chocolate chips
    Powdered sugar (optional)

Preheat oven to 350°F. Lightly grease
13×9-inch baking pan.

Place unsweetened chocolate, semisweet
chocolate and butter in medium microwavable
bowl. Microwave at HIGH 2 minutes or
until butter is melted; stir until chocolate is
completely melted. Cool to room temperature.

Place flour, salt and baking powder in small
bowl; stir to combine.

Beat sugar, eggs and vanilla in large bowl with
electric mixer at medium speed until slightly
thickened. Beat in chocolate mixture until well
combined. Add flour mixture; beat at low speed
until blended. Add sour cream; beat at low
speed until well blended. Stir in milk chocolate
chips. Spread mixture evenly in prepared pan.

Bake 20 to 25 minutes or until toothpick
inserted into center comes out almost clean.
(Do not overbake.) Cool brownies completely in
pan on wire rack. Cut into 2-inch squares. Place
powdered sugar in fine-mesh strainer; sprinkle
over brownies, if desired.

Store tightly covered at room temperature or
freeze up to 3 months.

Makes 2 dozen brownies

Caramel Oatmeal Chewies

1¾ cups quick or old-fashioned oats
1¾ cups all-purpose flour, *divided*
¾ cup packed brown sugar
½ teaspoon baking soda
¼ teaspoon salt (optional)
¾ cup (1½ sticks) butter or margarine,
    melted
2 cups (12-ounce package) NESTLÉ®
    TOLL HOUSE® Semi-Sweet
    Chocolate Morsels
1 cup chopped nuts
1 cup caramel ice-cream topping

PREHEAT oven to 350°F. Grease bottom of
13×9-inch baking pan.

COMBINE oats, *1½ cups* flour, brown sugar,
baking soda and salt in large bowl. Stir in
butter; mix well. Reserve *1 cup* oat mixture;
press *remaining* oat mixture onto bottom of
prepared baking pan.

BAKE for 12 to 15 minutes or until golden
brown. Sprinkle with morsels and nuts. Mix
caramel topping with *remaining* flour in small
bowl; drizzle over morsels to within ¼ inch of
pan edges. Sprinkle with *reserved* oat mixture.

BAKE for 18 to 22 minutes or until golden
brown. Cool in pan on wire rack; refrigerate
until firm. *Makes about 2½ dozen bars*

Caramel Oatmeal Chewies

Chocolate Cream Cheese Sugar Cookie Bars

1 package (22.3 ounces) golden sugar
    cookie mix
3 eggs, divided
⅓ cup plus 6 tablespoons butter or
    margarine, softened and divided
1 teaspoon water
1 package (8 ounces) cream cheese,
    softened
1 package (3 ounces) cream cheese,
    softened
¾ cup granulated sugar
⅓ cup HERSHEY₂S Cocoa
1½ teaspoons vanilla extract
    Powdered sugar

1. Heat oven to 350°F.

2. Empty cookie mix into large bowl. Break
up any lumps. Add 2 eggs, ⅓ cup butter
and water; stir with spoon or fork until well
blended. Spread into ungreased 13×9×2-inch
baking pan.

3. Beat cream cheese and remaining
6 tablespoons butter in medium bowl on
medium speed of mixer until fluffy. Stir
together granulated sugar and cocoa; gradually
add to cream cheese mixture, beating until
smooth and well blended. Add remaining egg
and vanilla; beat well. Spread cream cheese
mixture evenly over cookie batter.

4. Bake 35 to 40 minutes or until no imprint
remains when touched lightly in center. Cool
completely in pan on wire rack. Sprinkle
powdered sugar over top. Cut into bars. Cover;
store leftover bars in refrigerator.
Makes about 24 to 30 bars

Peanutty Cranberry Bars

½ cup (1 stick) butter or margarine,
    softened
½ cup granulated sugar
¼ cup packed light brown sugar
1 cup all-purpose flour
1 cup quick-cooking rolled oats
¼ teaspoon baking soda
¼ teaspoon salt
1 cup REESE'S® Peanut Butter Chips
1½ cups fresh or frozen whole
    cranberries
⅔ cup light corn syrup
½ cup water
1 teaspoon vanilla extract

1. Heat oven to 350°F. Grease 8-inch square
baking pan.

2. Beat butter, granulated sugar and brown
sugar in medium bowl until fluffy. Stir together
flour, oats, baking soda and salt; gradually add
to butter mixture, mixing until mixture is
consistency of coarse crumbs. Stir in peanut
butter chips.

3. Reserve 1½ cups mixture for crumb topping.
Firmly press remaining mixture evenly into
prepared pan. Bake 15 minutes or until set.
Meanwhile, in medium saucepan, combine
cranberries, corn syrup and water. Cook over
medium heat, stirring occasionally, until
mixture boils. Reduce heat; simmer 15 minutes,
stirring occasionally. Remove from heat. Stir
in vanilla. Spread evenly over baked layer.
Sprinkle reserved 1½ cups crumbs evenly
over top.

4. Return to oven. Bake 15 to 20 minutes or
until set. Cool completely in pan on wire rack.
Cut into bars. *Makes about 16 bars*

Chocolate Cream Cheese Sugar Cookie Bars

Golden Peanut Butter Bars

Prep Time: 20 minutes
Bake Time: 40 minutes

    2 cups all-purpose flour
    ¾ cup firmly packed light brown sugar
    1 egg, beaten
    ½ cup (1 stick) cold butter or
        margarine
    1 cup finely chopped peanuts
    1 (14-ounce) can EAGLE BRAND®
        Sweetened Condensed Milk
        (NOT evaporated milk)
    ½ cup peanut butter
    1 teaspoon vanilla extract

1. Preheat oven to 350°F. In large mixing bowl, combine flour, brown sugar and egg; cut in cold butter until crumbly. Stir in peanuts. Reserve 2 cups crumb mixture. Press remaining mixture on bottom of 13×9-inch baking pan.

2. Bake 15 minutes or until lightly browned.

3. Meanwhile, in another large mixing bowl, beat Eagle Brand, peanut butter and vanilla. Spread over prepared crust; top with reserved crumb mixture.

4. Bake an additional 25 minutes or until lightly browned. Cool. Cut into bars. Store covered at room temperature.

Makes 24 to 36 bars

Coconutty "M&M's"® Brownies

    6 squares (1 ounce each) semi-sweet
        chocolate
    ¾ cup granulated sugar
    ½ cup (1 stick) butter
    2 eggs
    1 tablespoon vegetable oil
    1 teaspoon vanilla extract
    1¼ cups all-purpose flour
    3 tablespoons unsweetened cocoa
        powder
    1 teaspoon baking powder
    ½ teaspoon salt
    1½ cups "M&M's"® Chocolate Mini
        Baking Bits, divided
    Coconut Topping (recipe follows)

Preheat oven to 350°F. Lightly grease 8×8×2-inch baking pan; set aside. In small saucepan combine chocolate, sugar and butter over low heat; stir constantly until chocolate is melted. Remove from heat; let cool slightly. In large bowl beat eggs, oil and vanilla; stir in chocolate mixture until well blended. In medium bowl combine flour, cocoa powder, baking powder and salt; add to chocolate mixture. Stir in 1 cup "M&M's"® Chocolate Mini Baking Bits. Spread batter evenly in prepared pan. Bake 35 to 40 minutes or until toothpick inserted in center comes out clean. Cool completely on wire rack. Prepare Coconut Topping. Spread over brownies; sprinkle with remaining ½ cup "M&M's"® Chocolate Mini Baking Bits. Cut into bars. Store in tightly covered container. *Makes 16 brownies*

Coconut Topping

    ½ cup (1 stick) butter
    ⅓ cup firmly packed light brown sugar
    ⅓ cup light corn syrup
    1 cup sweetened shredded coconut,
        toasted*
    ¾ cup chopped pecans
    1 teaspoon vanilla extract

*To toast coconut, spread evenly on cookie sheet. Toast in preheated 350°F oven 7 to 8 minutes or until golden brown, stirring occasionally.

In large saucepan melt butter over medium heat; add brown sugar and corn syrup, stirring constantly until thick and bubbly. Remove from heat and stir in remaining ingredients.

Golden Peanut Butter Bars

That Takes the Cake

Fudge Ribbon Cake

Prep Time: 20 minutes
Bake Time: 40 minutes

    1 (18.25-ounce) package chocolate cake mix
    1 (8-ounce) package cream cheese, softened
    2 tablespoons butter or margarine, softened
    1 tablespoon cornstarch
    1 (14-ounce) can EAGLE BRAND® Sweetened Condensed Milk (NOT evaporated
        milk)
    1 egg
    1 teaspoon vanilla extract
    Chocolate Glaze (recipe follows)

1. Preheat oven to 350°F. Grease and flour 13×9-inch baking pan. Prepare cake mix as package directs. Pour batter into prepared pan.

2. In small mixing bowl, beat cream cheese, butter and cornstarch until fluffy. Gradually beat in Eagle Brand. Add egg and vanilla; beat until smooth. Spoon evenly over cake batter.

3. Bake 40 minutes or until wooden pick inserted near center comes out clean. Cool. Prepare Chocolate Glaze and drizzle over cake. Store covered in refrigerator.   *Makes 10 to 12 servings*

Chocolate Glaze: In small saucepan over low heat, melt 1 (1-ounce) square unsweetened or semi-sweet chocolate and 1 tablespoon butter or margarine with 2 tablespoons water. Remove from heat. Stir in ¾ cup powdered sugar and ½ teaspoon vanilla extract. Stir until smooth and well blended. Makes about ⅓ cup.

Fudge Ribbon Bundt Cake: Preheat oven to 350°F. Grease and flour 10-inch Bundt pan. Prepare cake mix as package directs. Pour batter into prepared pan. Prepare cream cheese layer as directed above; spoon evenly over batter. Bake 50 to 55 minutes or until wooden pick inserted near center comes out clean. Cool 10 minutes. Remove from pan. Cool. Prepare Chocolate Glaze and drizzle over cake. Store covered in refrigerator.

Fudge Ribbon Cake

Sock-It-To-Me Cake

Streusel Filling
- 1 package DUNCAN HINES® Moist Deluxe® Butter Recipe Golden Cake Mix, divided
- 2 tablespoons brown sugar
- 2 teaspoons ground cinnamon
- 1 cup finely chopped pecans

Cake
- 4 eggs
- 1 cup dairy sour cream
- ⅓ cup vegetable oil
- ¼ cup water
- ¼ cup granulated sugar

Glaze
- 1 cup confectioners' sugar
- 1 or 2 tablespoons milk

1. Preheat oven to 375°F. Grease and flour 10-inch tube pan.

2. For streusel filling, combine 2 tablespoons cake mix, brown sugar and cinnamon in medium bowl. Stir in pecans. Set aside.

3. For cake, combine remaining cake mix, eggs, sour cream, oil, water and granulated sugar in large bowl. Beat at medium speed with electric mixer 2 minutes. Pour two-thirds of batter into prepared pan. Sprinkle with streusel filling. Spoon remaining batter evenly over filling. Bake at 375°F for 45 to 55 minutes or until toothpick inserted in center comes out clean. Cool in pan 25 minutes. Invert onto serving plate. Cool completely.

4. For glaze, combine confectioners' sugar and milk in small bowl. Stir until smooth. Drizzle over cake.   *Makes 12 to 16 servings*

Tip: For a quick glaze, place ½ cup Duncan Hines® Creamy Homestyle Vanilla Frosting in small microwave-safe bowl. Microwave at HIGH (100% power) 10 seconds; add 5 to 10 seconds, if needed. Stir until smooth and thin.

Karen Ann's Lemon Cake

- 2 cups all-purpose flour
- 1½ teaspoons baking powder
- ½ teaspoon baking soda
- ¼ teaspoon salt
- ⅔ cup butter or margarine, softened
- 1¼ cups granulated sugar
- 3 eggs, separated
- ¾ cup sour cream
- Grated peel of 1 SUNKIST® lemon
- Lemony Frosting (recipe follows)

Line two 8-inch round cake pans with waxed paper. Preheat oven to 350°F. In medium bowl, combine flour, baking powder, baking soda and salt. In large bowl, with electric mixer, cream butter and sugar. Beat in egg yolks one at a time; beat until light in color. Add flour mixture alternately with sour cream, beating just until smooth. In separate bowl, with clean beaters, beat egg whites until soft peaks form. Fold beaten egg whites and lemon peel into batter. Pour batter into prepared pans. Bake at 350°F for 30 to 35 minutes or until wooden pick inserted in center comes out clean. Cool 10 minutes. Remove from pans and peel off waxed paper. Cool on wire racks. Fill and frost with Lemony Frosting.   *Makes 12 servings*

Lemony Frosting

- ½ cup butter or margarine, softened
- 3 cups confectioners' sugar, divided
- Grated peel of ½ SUNKIST® lemon
- 2 tablespoons fresh squeezed SUNKIST® lemon juice

In medium bowl, cream together butter and 1 cup confectioners' sugar. Add lemon peel, lemon juice and remaining 2 cups sugar; beat until smooth.   *Makes about 1¾ cups frosting*

Sock-It-To-Me Cake

Fresh Apple Cake

3 cups flour, divided
3 cups finely chopped apples
1 cup finely chopped pecans or walnuts
3 eggs *or* ¾ cup egg substitute
2 cups sugar
1 cup vegetable oil
2 teaspoons ground cinnamon
2 teaspoons vanilla
1 teaspoon ARM & HAMMER® Baking
   Soda
1 teaspoon nutmeg
½ teaspoon salt

Toss ¼ cup flour with apples and nuts. Beat eggs thoroughly in large bowl; blend in sugar. Alternately add remaining 2¾ cups flour and oil. Stir in cinnamon, vanilla, Baking Soda, nutmeg and salt; mix well. Fold in apple mixture. Pour batter into greased and floured 10-inch tube pan. Bake at 350°F 1 hour.

Makes 16 servings

Butterscotch Banana Cake

1⅔ cups (11-ounce package) NESTLÉ®
   TOLL HOUSE® Butterscotch
   Flavored Morsels, *divided*
1 package (18.5 ounces) yellow cake
   mix
4 eggs
¾ cup (2 medium) mashed ripe bananas
½ cup vegetable oil
¼ cup water
¼ cup granulated sugar

PREHEAT oven to 375°F. Grease 10-cup bundt or round tube pan.

MICROWAVE *1⅓ cups* morsels in medium, microwave-safe bowl on MEDIUM-HIGH (70%) power for 1 minute; stir. Microwave at additional 10- to 20-second intervals, stirring until smooth. Combine cake mix, eggs, bananas, vegetable oil, water and granulated sugar in large mixer bowl. Beat on low speed until moistened. Beat on high speed for 2 minutes. Stir *2 cups* batter into melted morsels. Alternately spoon batters into prepared bundt or round tube pan.

BAKE for 35 to 45 minutes or until wooden pick inserted in cake comes out clean. Cool in pan for 20 minutes; invert onto wire rack to cool completely.

PLACE *remaining* morsels in small, *heavy-duty* plastic bag. Microwave on MEDIUM-HIGH (70%) power for 30 seconds; knead. Microwave at additional 10- to 20-second intervals, kneading until smooth. Cut tiny corner from bag; squeeze to drizzle over cake.

Makes 24 servings

Mini Turtle Cupcakes

1 package (21½ ounces) brownie mix
   plus ingredients to prepare mix
½ cup chopped pecans
1 cup prepared or homemade dark
   chocolate frosting
½ cup coarsely chopped pecans, toasted
12 caramels, unwrapped
1 to 2 tablespoons whipping cream

1. Heat oven to 350°F. Line 54 mini (1½-inch) muffin cups with paper baking cups.

2. Prepare brownie batter as directed on package. Stir in chopped pecans.

3. Spoon batter into prepared muffin cups filling ⅔ full. Bake 18 minutes or until toothpicks inserted into centers come out clean. Cool in pans on wire racks 5 minutes. Remove cupcakes to racks; cool completely. (At this point, cupcakes may be frozen up to 3 months. Thaw at room temperature before frosting.)

4. Spread frosting over cooled cupcakes; top with toasted pecans.

5. Combine caramels and 1 tablespoon cream in small saucepan. Cook and stir over low heat until caramels are melted and mixture is smooth. Add additional 1 tablespoon cream if needed. Spoon caramel over cupcakes. Store at room temperature up to 24 hours or cover and refrigerate for up to 3 days before serving.

Makes 54 mini cupcakes

Mini Turtle Cupcakes

Sour Cream Pound Cake

1 orange
1 cup butter, softened
2¾ cups sugar
1 tablespoon vanilla
6 eggs
3 cups all-purpose flour
½ teaspoon salt
¼ teaspoon baking soda
1 cup sour cream
Citrus Topping (recipe follows)

Preheat oven to 325°F. Grease 10-inch tube pan. Finely grate peel of orange (not white pith) to measure 2 teaspoons; set aside. Beat butter in large bowl with electric mixer at medium speed until creamy, scraping down side of bowl once. Gradually add sugar, beating until light and fluffy. Beat in vanilla and orange peel. Add eggs, 1 at a time, beating 1 minute after each addition. Combine flour, salt and baking soda in small bowl. Add to butter mixture alternately with sour cream, beginning and ending with flour mixture. Beat well after each addition. Pour into prepared pan. Bake 1 hour 15 minutes or until toothpick inserted near center comes out clean.

Meanwhile, prepare Citrus Topping. Spoon over hot cake; cool in pan 15 minutes. Remove from pan to wire rack; cool completely.

Makes 10 to 12 servings

Citrus Topping

2 oranges
2 teaspoons salt
Water
½ cup sugar, divided
⅓ cup lemon juice
1 teaspoon vanilla

Grate peel of oranges (not white pith) to measure ⅓ cup. Cut oranges in half. Squeeze juice from oranges to measure ⅓ cup. Combine orange peel and salt in medium saucepan. Add enough water to cover. Bring to a boil over high heat. Boil 2 minutes. Drain in fine-meshed sieve. Return orange peel to saucepan. Add orange juice and ¼ cup sugar to saucepan. Bring to a boil over high heat. Reduce heat;

simmer 10 minutes. Remove from heat. Add remaining ¼ cup sugar, lemon juice and vanilla; stir until smooth.

Chocolate Syrup Swirl Cake

1 cup (2 sticks) butter or margarine, softened
2 cups sugar
2 teaspoons vanilla extract
3 eggs
2¾ cups all-purpose flour
1¼ teaspoons baking soda, divided
½ teaspoon salt
1 cup buttermilk or sour milk*
1 cup HERSHEY₅S Syrup
1 cup MOUNDS® Sweetened Coconut Flakes (optional)

*To sour milk: Use 1 tablespoon white vinegar plus milk to equal 1 cup.

1. Heat oven to 350°F. Grease and flour 12-cup fluted tube pan or 10-inch tube pan.

2. Beat butter, sugar and vanilla in large bowl until fluffy. Add eggs; beat well. Stir together flour, 1 teaspoon baking soda and salt; add alternately with buttermilk to butter mixture, beating until well blended.

3. Measure 2 cups batter in small bowl; stir in syrup and remaining ¼ teaspoon baking soda. Add coconut, if desired, to remaining batter; pour into prepared pan. Pour chocolate batter over vanilla batter in pan; do not mix.

4. Bake 60 to 70 minutes or until wooden pick inserted in center comes out clean. Cool 15 minutes; remove from pan to wire rack. Cool completely on wire rack; glaze or frost as desired.

Makes 20 servings

Chocolate Syrup Swirl Cake

Blueberry Crisp Cupcakes

Cupcakes
2 cups all-purpose flour
2 teaspoons baking powder
¼ teaspoon salt
1¾ cups granulated sugar
½ cup (1 stick) butter, softened
¾ cup milk
1½ teaspoons vanilla
3 egg whites
3 cups fresh or frozen (unthawed)
    blueberries

Streusel
⅓ cup all-purpose flour
¼ cup uncooked old-fashioned or quick
    oats
¼ cup packed light brown sugar
½ teaspoon ground cinnamon
¼ cup butter, softened
½ cup chopped walnuts or pecans

1. Preheat oven to 350°F. Line 30 regular-size (2½-inch) muffin cups with paper baking cups.

2. For cupcakes, combine 2 cups flour, baking powder and salt in medium bowl; mix well and set aside. Beat granulated sugar and ½ cup butter with electric mixer at medium speed 1 minute. Add milk and vanilla. Beat at low speed 30 seconds. Gradually beat in flour mixture; beat at medium speed 2 minutes. Add egg whites; beat 1 minute. Spoon batter into prepared muffin cups filling half full. Spoon blueberries over batter. Bake 10 minutes.

3. Meanwhile for streusel, combine ⅓ cup flour, oats, brown sugar and cinnamon in small bowl; mix well. Cut in ¼ cup butter with pastry blender or two knives until mixture is well combined. Stir in chopped nuts.

4. Sprinkle streusel over partially baked cupcakes. Return to oven; bake 18 to 20 minutes or until golden brown and toothpicks inserted into centers come out clean. Cool in pans on wire racks 10 minutes. Remove cupcakes to racks; cool completely. (Cupcakes may be frozen up to 3 months.)
Makes 30 cupcakes

Southern Jam Cake

Cake
¾ cup butter or margarine, softened
1 cup granulated sugar
3 eggs
1 cup (12-ounce jar) SMUCKER'S®
    Seedless Blackberry Jam
2½ cups all-purpose flour
1 teaspoon baking soda
1 teaspoon ground cinnamon
1 teaspoon ground cloves
1 teaspoon ground allspice
1 teaspoon ground nutmeg
¾ cup buttermilk

Caramel Icing (optional)
2 tablespoons butter
½ cup firmly packed brown sugar
3 tablespoons milk
1¾ cups powdered sugar

Grease and flour tube pan. Combine ¾ cup butter and granulated sugar; beat until light and fluffy. Add eggs one at a time, beating well after each addition. Fold in jam.

Combine flour, baking soda, cinnamon, cloves, allspice and nutmeg; mix well. Add to batter alternately with buttermilk, stirring just enough to blend after each addition. Spoon mixture into prepared pan.

Bake at 350°F for 50 minutes or until toothpick inserted in center comes out clean. Cool in pan for 10 minutes. Remove from pan; cool completely.

In saucepan, melt 2 tablespoons butter; stir in brown sugar. Cook, stirring constantly, until mixture boils; remove from heat. Cool 5 minutes. Stir in milk; blend in powdered sugar. Frost cake.   *Makes 12 to 16 servings*

Blueberry Crisp Cupcakes

Rich & Gooey Apple-Caramel Cake

Cake

    PAM® No-Stick Cooking Spray
2 cups all-purpose flour
1 teaspoon salt
1 teaspoon baking soda
1 teaspoon pumpkin pie spice
1½ cups sugar
  ¾ cup WESSON® Vegetable Oil
3 eggs
2 teaspoons vanilla
3 cups peeled, cored and sliced tart
    apples, such as Granny Smith
    (½-inch slices)
1 cup chopped walnuts

Glaze

  1 cup firmly packed light brown sugar
  ½ cup (1 stick) butter
  ¼ cup milk
    Whipped cream

For cake, preheat oven to 350°F. Spray 13×9×2-inch baking pan with PAM® Cooking Spray; set aside. In medium bowl, combine flour, salt, baking soda and pie spice; mix well. Set aside. In large bowl, with electric mixer, beat sugar, Wesson® Oil, eggs and vanilla for 3 minutes at medium speed. Add flour mixture and stir until dry ingredients are moistened; fold in apples and walnuts. Pour batter into baking pan and spread evenly; bake 50 to 55 minutes or until wooden pick inserted into center comes out clean. Cool cake in pan on wire rack.

Meanwhile, for glaze, in small saucepan over medium heat, bring brown sugar, butter and milk to a boil, stirring until sugar has dissolved. Boil 1 minute. Spoon half of glaze over warm cake; set *remaining* aside. Allow cake to stand 5 minutes. Top *each* serving with *remaining* glaze and whipped cream.

Makes 12 to 15 servings

Refreshing Choco-Orange Cheesecake

1 cup graham cracker crumbs
¼ cup (½ stick) butter or margarine,
    melted
2 cups sugar, divided
1 cup HERSHEY®S Semi-Sweet
    Chocolate Chips
3 packages (8 ounces each) cream
    cheese, softened
4 eggs
1½ cups dairy sour cream
2 teaspoons orange extract
1 teaspoon freshly grated orange peel
    Whipped topping
    Orange wedges (optional)

1. Stir together graham cracker crumbs, melted butter and ¼ cup sugar in small bowl; pat firmly on bottom of 9-inch springform pan.

2. Place chocolate chips in medium microwave-safe bowl. Microwave at HIGH (100%) 1 minute or just until chips are melted when stirred.

3. Beat cream cheese and remaining 1¾ cups sugar in large bowl; add eggs, one at a time, beating after each addition. Stir in sour cream and orange extract. Stir 3 cups cream cheese mixture into melted chocolate chips; pour into crust. Freeze 10 to 15 minutes or until chocolate sets.

4. Heat oven to 325°F. Stir orange peel into remaining cream cheese mixture; gently spread over chocolate mixture.

5. Bake 1 hour 15 minutes or until set except for 3-inch circle in center; turn off oven. Let stand in oven, with door ajar, 1 hour; remove from oven. With knife, loosen cheesecake from side of pan. Cool completely; remove side of pan. Cover; refrigerate. Garnish with whipped topping and orange wedges, if desired. Cover; refrigerate leftover cheesecake.

Makes 12 servings

Rich & Gooey Apple-Caramel Cake

Glazed Chocolate Pound Cake

Prep Time: about 30 minutes
Bake Time: 75 to 85 minutes

Cake

1¾ Butter Flavor CRISCO® Sticks or
  1¾ cups Butter Flavor CRISCO®
  all-vegetable shortening plus
  additional for greasing
3 cups granulated sugar
5 eggs
1 teaspoon vanilla
3¼ cups all-purpose flour
½ cup unsweetened cocoa powder
1 teaspoon baking powder
½ teaspoon salt
1⅓ cups milk
1 cup miniature semisweet chocolate
  chips

Glaze

1 cup miniature semisweet chocolate
  chips
¼ Butter Flavor CRISCO® Stick or
  ¼ cup Butter Flavor CRISCO®
  all-vegetable shortening
1 tablespoon light corn syrup

1. For cake, heat oven to 325°F. Grease and flour 10-inch tube pan.

2. Combine 1¾ cups shortening, sugar, eggs and vanilla in large bowl. Beat at low speed with electric mixer until blended, scraping bowl frequently. Beat at high speed 6 minutes, scraping bowl occasionally. Combine flour, cocoa, baking powder and salt in medium bowl. Mix in dry ingredients alternately with milk, beating after each addition until batter is smooth. Stir in 1 cup chocolate chips. Spoon into prepared pan.

3. Bake at 325°F for 75 to 85 minutes or until toothpick inserted near center comes out clean. Cool on cooling rack 20 minutes. Invert onto serving dish. Cool completely.

4. For glaze, combine 1 cup chocolate chips, ¼ cup shortening and corn syrup in top part of double boiler over hot, not boiling, water. Stir until just melted and smooth. Cool slightly. (Or place mixture in microwave-safe bowl.

Microwave at 50% (Medium) power for 1 minute and 15 seconds. Stir. Repeat at 15-second intervals, if necessary, until just melted and smooth. Cool slightly.) Spoon glaze over cake. Let stand until glaze is firm.

Makes 1 (10-inch) tube cake

Cookies & Cream Cupcakes

2¼ cups all-purpose flour
1 tablespoon baking powder
½ teaspoon salt
1⅔ cups sugar
1 cup milk
½ cup (1 stick) butter, softened
2 teaspoons vanilla
3 egg whites
1 cup crushed chocolate sandwich
  cookies (about 10 cookies) plus
  additional for garnish
1 container (16 ounces) vanilla frosting

1. Preheat oven to 350°F. Line 24 regular-size (2½-inch) muffin pan cups with paper baking cups.

2. Sift flour, baking powder and salt together in large bowl. Stir in sugar. Add milk, butter and vanilla; beat with electric mixer at low speed 30 seconds. Beat at medium speed 2 minutes. Add egg whites; beat 2 minutes. Stir in 1 cup crushed cookies.

3. Spoon batter into prepared muffin cups. Bake 20 to 25 minutes or until toothpicks inserted into centers come out clean. Cool in pans on wire racks 10 minutes. Remove to racks; cool completely.

4. Frost cupcakes; garnish with additional crushed cookies. *Makes 24 cupcakes*

Cookies & Cream Cupcakes

Chocolate Peanut Butter Cups

1 package DUNCAN HINES® Moist
   Deluxe® Swiss Chocolate Cake Mix
1 container DUNCAN HINES® Creamy
   Home-Style Classic Vanilla
   Frosting
½ cup creamy peanut butter
15 miniature peanut butter cup candies,
   wrappers removed, cut in half
   vertically

1. Preheat oven to 350°F. Place 30 (2½-inch) paper liners in muffin cups.

2. Prepare, bake and cool cupcakes following package directions for basic recipe.

3. Combine Vanilla frosting and peanut butter in medium bowl. Stir until smooth. Frost one cupcake. Decorate with peanut butter cup candy, cut side down. Repeat with remaining cupcakes, frosting and candies.   *Makes 30 servings*

Golden Apple Cupcakes

1 package (18 to 20 ounces) yellow cake
   mix
1 cup MOTT'S® Chunky Apple Sauce
⅓ cup vegetable oil
3 eggs
¼ cup firmly packed light brown sugar
¼ cup chopped walnuts
½ teaspoon ground cinnamon
   Vanilla Frosting (recipe follows)

Heat oven to 350°F. In bowl, combine cake mix, apple sauce, oil and eggs; blend according to package directions. Spoon batter into 24 paper-lined muffin pan cups. Mix brown sugar, walnuts and cinnamon; sprinkle over prepared batter in muffin cups. Bake 20 to 25 minutes or until toothpick inserted in center comes out clean. Cool in pan 10 minutes. Remove from pan; cool completely on wire rack. Frost cupcakes with Vanilla Frosting.
     Makes 24 cupcakes

Vanilla Frosting: In large bowl, beat 1 package (8 ounces) softened cream cheese until light and creamy; blend in ¼ teaspoon vanilla extract. Beat ½ cup heavy cream until stiff; fold into cream cheese mixture.

Hershey's Red Velvet Cake

½ cup (1 stick) butter or margarine,
   softened
1½ cups sugar
2 eggs
1 teaspoon vanilla extract
1 cup buttermilk or sour milk*
2 tablespoons (1-ounce bottle) red food
   color
2 cups all-purpose flour
⅓ cup HERSHEY'S Cocoa
1 teaspoon salt
1½ teaspoons baking soda
1 tablespoon white vinegar
1 can (16 ounces) ready-to-spread
   vanilla frosting
   HERSHEY'S MINI CHIPS™
   Semi-Sweet Chocolate Chips or
   HERSHEY'S Milk Chocolate Chips
   (optional)

To sour milk: Use 1 tablespoon white vinegar plus milk to equal 1 cup.

1. Heat oven to 350°F. Grease and flour 13×9×2-inch baking pan.**

2. Beat butter and sugar in large bowl; add eggs and vanilla, beating well. Stir together buttermilk and food color. Stir together flour, cocoa and salt; add alternately to butter mixture with buttermilk mixture, mixing well. Stir in baking soda and vinegar. Pour into prepared pan.

3. Bake 30 to 35 minutes or until wooden pick inserted in center comes out clean. Cool completely in pan on wire rack. Frost; garnish with chocolate chips, if desired.
     Makes about 15 servings

**This recipe can be made in 2 (9-inch) cake pans. Bake at 350°F for 30 to 35 minutes.*

Chocolate Peanut Butter Cups

Country Oat Cake

Cake

    1 package (18.5 ounces) spice cake mix
    1 cup QUAKER® Oats (quick or old fashioned, uncooked)
    1 carton (8 ounces) plain lowfat yogurt
    3 eggs or ¾ cup egg substitute
    ¼ cup vegetable oil
    ¼ cup water
    1½ cups peeled, finely chopped apples (about 2 medium)

Topping

    1 cup QUAKER® Oats (quick or old fashioned, uncooked)
    ½ cup firmly packed brown sugar
    ¼ cup (½ stick) margarine or butter, softened
    ½ teaspoon ground cinnamon
    Whipped cream (optional)

Heat oven to 350°F. Grease and flour 13×9-inch baking pan. For cake, combine cake mix, oats, yogurt, eggs, oil and water. Blend on low speed of electric mixer until moistened; mix at medium speed for 2 minutes. Stir in apples. Pour into prepared pan. For topping, combine oats, brown sugar, margarine and cinnamon; mix well. Sprinkle evenly over batter. Bake 40 to 45 minutes or until wooden pick inserted in center comes out clean. Serve warm or at room temperature with whipped cream, if desired. *Makes 16 servings*

Chocolate Raspberry Cheesecake

Prep Time: 15 minutes
Chilling Time: 3 hours

    2 (3-ounce) packages cream cheese, softened
    1 (14-ounce) can sweetened condensed milk
    1 egg
    3 tablespoons lemon juice
    1 teaspoon vanilla
    1 cup fresh or frozen raspberries
    1 (6-ounce) READY CRUST® Chocolate Pie Crust
    Chocolate Glaze (recipe follows)

1. Preheat oven to 350°F. Beat cream cheese in medium bowl with electric mixer at medium speed until fluffy. Gradually beat in sweetened condensed milk until smooth. Add egg, lemon juice and vanilla; mix well. Arrange raspberries on bottom of crust. Slowly pour cream cheese mixture over raspberries.

2. Bake 30 to 35 minutes or until center is almost set. Cool on wire rack.

3 . Prepare Chocolate Glaze; spread over cheesecake. Refrigerate 3 hours. Garnish as desired. Refrigerate leftovers.

Makes 8 servings

Chocolate Glaze: Melt 2 (1-ounce) squares semisweet baking chocolate with ¼ cup whipping cream in small saucepan over low heat. Cook and stir until thickened and smooth. Remove from heat.

Chocolate Raspberry Cheesecake

Double Malted Cupcakes

Cupcakes
        2 cups all-purpose flour
        ¼ cup malted milk powder
        2 teaspoons baking powder
        ¼ teaspoon salt
        1¾ cups granulated sugar
        ½ cup (1 stick) butter, softened
        1 cup 2% or whole milk
        1½ teaspoons vanilla
        3 egg whites

Frosting
        4 ounces milk chocolate candy bar,
            broken into chunks
        ¼ cup (½ stick) butter
        ¼ cup whipping cream
        1 tablespoon malted milk powder
        1 teaspoon vanilla
        1¾ cups powdered sugar
        30 chocolate-covered malt ball candies

1. Preheat oven to 350°F. Line 30 regular-size (2½-inch) muffin cups with paper baking cups.

2. For cupcakes, combine flour, ¼ cup malted milk powder, baking powder and salt; mix well and set aside. Beat sugar and ½ cup butter with electric mixer at medium speed 1 minute. Add milk and 1½ teaspoons vanilla. Beat at low speed 30 seconds. Gradually beat in flour mixture; beat at medium speed 2 minutes. Add egg whites; beat 1 minute.

3. Spoon batter into prepared muffin cups filling ⅔ full. Bake 20 minutes or until golden brown and toothpicks inserted into centers come out clean. Cool in pans on wire racks 10 minutes. (Centers of cupcakes will sink slightly upon cooling.) Remove cupcakes to racks; cool completely. (At this point, cupcakes may be frozen up to 3 months.)

4. For frosting, melt chocolate and ¼ cup butter in heavy medium saucepan over low heat, stirring frequently. Stir in cream, 1 tablespoon malted milk powder and 1 teaspoon vanilla; mix well. Gradually stir in powdered sugar. Cook 4 to 5 minutes, stirring constantly, until small lumps disappear. Remove from heat. Chill 20 minutes, beating every 5 minutes until frosting is spreadable.

5. Spread cooled cupcakes with frosting; decorate with chocolate covered malt ball candies. Store at room temperature up to 24 hours or cover and refrigerate for up to 3 days before serving.   *Makes 30 cupcakes*

Carrot Layer Cake

Cake
        1 package DUNCAN HINES® Moist
            Deluxe® Classic Yellow Cake Mix
        4 eggs
        ½ cup vegetable oil
        3 cups grated carrots
        1 cup finely chopped nuts
        2 teaspoons ground cinnamon

Cream Cheese Frosting
        1 package (8 ounces) cream cheese,
            softened
        ¼ cup butter or margarine, softened
        2 teaspoons vanilla extract
        4 cups confectioners' sugar

1. Preheat oven to 350°F. Grease and flour two 8- or 9-inch round baking pans.

2. For cake, combine cake mix, eggs, oil, carrots, nuts and cinnamon in large bowl. Beat at low speed with electric mixer until moistened. Beat at medium speed for 2 minutes. Pour into prepared pans. Bake at 350°F for 35 to 40 minutes or until toothpick inserted in centers comes out clean. Cool.

3. For cream cheese frosting, place cream cheese, butter and vanilla extract in large bowl. Beat at low speed until smooth and creamy. Add confectioners' sugar gradually, beating until smooth. Add more sugar to thicken, or milk or water to thin frosting, as needed. Fill and frost cooled cake. Garnish with whole pecans.   *Makes 12 to 16 servings*

Carrot Layer Cake

Fudgy Peanut Butter Cake

1 (18.25-ounce) box chocolate fudge
    cake mix
2 eggs
1½ cups plus ⅔ cup water, divided
1 (16-ounce) package chocolate fudge
    frosting mix
1¼ cups SMUCKER'S® Chunky Natural
    Peanut Butter or JIF® Chunky
    Peanut Butter

Grease and flour 10-inch tube pan. In large
bowl, blend cake mix, eggs and 1½ cups water
until moistened; mix as directed on cake mix
package. Pour batter into pan.

In medium bowl, combine frosting mix, peanut
butter and remaining ⅔ cup water; blend until
smooth. Spoon over batter in pan.

Bake in preheated 350°F oven 35 to 45 minutes
or until top springs back when touched lightly
in center. Cool upright in pan 1 hour; remove
from pan. Cool completely.

Makes 12 to 15 servings

Cappuccino Cupcakes

1 package (about 18 ounces) dark
    chocolate cake mix
1⅓ cups strong brewed or instant coffee,
    at room temperature
3 eggs
⅓ cup vegetable oil or melted butter
1 container (16 ounces) prepared
    vanilla frosting
2 tablespoons coffee liqueur
    Additional coffee liqueur (optional)
    Grated chocolate*
    Chocolate-covered coffee beans
    (optional)

**Grate half of a 3- or 4-ounce milk, dark or espresso
chocolate candy bar on the large holes of a grater.*

1. Preheat oven to 350°F. Line 24 regular-size
(2½-inch) muffin cups with foil or paper baking
cups.

2. Beat cake mix, coffee, eggs and oil with
electric mixer at low speed 30 seconds. Beat at
medium speed 2 minutes.

3. Spoon batter into prepared muffin cups
filling ⅔ full. Bake 18 to 20 minutes or until
toothpicks inserted into centers come out clean.
Cool in pans on wire racks 10 minutes. Remove
cupcakes to racks; cool completely. (At this
point, cupcakes may be frozen up to 3 months.
Thaw at room temperature before frosting.)

4. Combine frosting and 2 tablespoons liqueur
in small bowl; mix well. Before frosting, poke
about 10 holes in each cupcake with toothpick.
Pour 1 to 2 teaspoons liqueur over top of each
cupcake, if desired. Frost and sprinkle with
grated chocolate. Garnish with chocolate-
covered coffee beans, if desired.

Makes 24 cupcakes

Quick & Easy Chocolate Cake

4 bars (1 ounce each) HERSHEY'S
    Unsweetened Baking Chocolate,
    broken into pieces
¼ cup (½ stick) butter or margarine
1⅔ cups boiling water
2⅓ cups all-purpose flour
2 cups sugar
½ cup dairy sour cream
2 eggs
2 teaspoons baking soda
1 teaspoon salt
1 teaspoon vanilla extract

1. Heat oven to 350°F. Grease and flour
13×9×2-inch baking pan.

2. Combine chocolate, butter and water in
large bowl; with spoon, stir until chocolate is
melted and mixture is smooth. Add flour, sugar,
sour cream, eggs, baking soda, salt and vanilla;
beat on low speed of mixer until smooth. Pour
batter into prepared pan.

3. Bake 35 to 40 minutes or until wooden
pick inserted in center comes out clean. Cool
completely in pan on wire rack. Frost as
desired.   *Makes 12 to 15 servings*

Cappuccino Cupcakes

German Chocolate Cake

Prep Time: 15 minutes
Bake Time: 40 to 45 minutes

    1 (18.25-ounce) package chocolate cake
       mix
    1 cup water
    3 eggs
    ½ cup vegetable oil
    1 (14-ounce) can EAGLE BRAND®
       Sweetened Condensed Milk
       (NOT evaporated milk), divided
    3 tablespoons butter or margarine
    1 egg yolk
    ⅓ cup chopped pecans
    ⅓ cup flaked coconut
    1 teaspoon vanilla extract

1. Preheat oven to 350°F. Grease and flour
13×9-inch baking pan. In large mixing bowl,
combine cake mix, water, 3 eggs, oil and ⅓ cup
Eagle Brand. Beat at low speed of electric
mixer until moistened; beat at high speed
2 minutes.

2. Pour into prepared pan. Bake 40 to
45 minutes or until wooden pick inserted near
center comes out clean.

3. In small saucepan over medium heat,
combine remaining Eagle Brand, butter and
egg yolk. Cook and stir until thickened, about
6 minutes. Add pecans, coconut and vanilla;
spread over warm cake. Store covered in
refrigerator.   *Makes 10 to 12 servings*

Chocolate-Raspberry Cupcakes

    2 cups all-purpose flour
    ⅔ cup unsweetened cocoa powder
    1¾ teaspoons baking soda
    ½ teaspoon baking powder
    ½ teaspoon salt
    1¾ cups granulated sugar
    ⅔ cup vegetable shortening
    1 cup cold water
    2 teaspoons vanilla extract
    3 eggs
    ⅓ cup seedless raspberry jam
    1½ cups "M&M's"® Semi-Sweet
       Chocolate Mini Baking Bits,
       divided
    1 container (16 ounces) white frosting
       Red food coloring

Preheat oven to 350°F. Lightly grease
24 (2¾-inch) muffin cups or line with paper
or foil liners; set aside. In large bowl combine
flour, cocoa powder, baking soda, baking powder
and salt; stir in sugar. Beat in shortening until
well combined. Gradually beat in water; stir in
vanilla. Beat in eggs. Stir in raspberry jam.
Divide batter evenly among prepared muffin
cups. Sprinkle batter with 1 cup "M&M's"®
Semi-Sweet Chocolate Mini Baking Bits. Bake
20 to 25 minutes or until toothpick inserted
in centers comes out clean. Cool completely
on wire racks. Combine frosting and red food
coloring to make frosting pink. Spread frosting
over cupcakes; decorate with remaining
½ cup "M&M's"® Semi-Sweet Chocolate Mini
Baking Bits. Store in tightly covered container.
    Makes 24 cupcakes

German Chocolate Cake

Banana Split Cupcakes

1 package (about 18 ounces) yellow
    cake mix, divided
1 cup water
1 cup mashed ripe bananas
3 eggs
1 cup chopped drained maraschino
    cherries
1½ cups miniature semisweet chocolate
    chips, divided
1½ cups prepared vanilla frosting
1 cup marshmallow creme
1 teaspoon shortening
30 whole maraschino cherries, drained
    and patted dry

1. Preheat oven to 350°F. Line 30 regular-size
(2½-inch) muffin cups with paper baking cups.

2. Reserve 2 tablespoons cake mix. Combine
remaining cake mix, water, bananas and eggs in
large bowl. Beat at low speed of electric mixer
until moistened, about 30 seconds. Beat at
medium speed 2 minutes. Combine chopped
cherries and reserved cake mix in small bowl.
Stir chopped cherry mixture and 1 cup
chocolate chips into batter.

3. Spoon batter into prepared muffin cups.
Bake 15 to 20 minutes or until toothpicks
inserted into centers come out clean. Cool in
pans on wire racks 10 minutes. Remove to wire
racks; cool completely.

4. Combine frosting and marshmallow creme
in medium bowl until well blended. Frost
cupcakes.

5. Combine remaining ½ cup chocolate chips
and shortening in small microwavable bowl.
Microwave at HIGH 30 to 45 seconds, stirring
after 30 seconds, or until smooth. Drizzle
chocolate mixture over cupcakes. Place one
whole cherry on each cupcake.

Makes 30 cupcakes

Note: If desired, omit chocolate drizzle and top
cupcakes with colored sprinkles.

Pineapple Orange Pound Cake

1 package DUNCAN HINES® Moist
    Deluxe® Pineapple Supreme Cake
    Mix
1 (4-serving size) package vanilla-
    flavor instant pudding and pie
    filling mix
4 eggs
1 cup plus 4 tablespoons orange juice,
    divided
⅓ cup vegetable oil
1 tablespoon grated orange peel
⅓ cup granulated sugar

Preheat oven to 350°F. Grease and flour 10-inch
Bundt pan.

Combine cake mix, pudding mix, eggs, 1 cup
orange juice, oil and orange peel in large mixing
bowl. Beat at medium speed with electric mixer
for 2 minutes. Pour into prepared pan. Bake
50 to 60 minutes or until toothpick inserted in
center comes out clean. Cool 25 minutes in pan.
Invert onto serving plate.

Combine sugar and 4 tablespoons orange juice
in small saucepan. Simmer 3 minutes. Brush
warm glaze on cake.

Makes 12 to 16 servings

Banana Split Cupcakes

Reese's® Chocolate Peanut Butter Cheesecake

1¼ cups graham cracker crumbs
⅓ cup plus ¼ cup sugar
⅓ cup HERSHEY®S Cocoa
⅓ cup butter or margarine, melted
3 packages (8 ounces each) cream cheese, softened
1 can (14 ounces) sweetened condensed milk (not evaporated milk)
1⅔ cup (10-ounce package) REESE'S® Peanut Butter Chips, melted
4 eggs
2 teaspoons vanilla extract
Chocolate Drizzle (recipe follows)
Whipped topping
HERSHEY®S MINI KISSES™ Semi-Sweet or Milk Chocolates

1. Heat oven to 300°F. Combine graham cracker crumbs, ⅓ cup sugar, cocoa and butter; press onto bottom of 9-inch springform pan.

2. Beat cream cheese and remaining ¼ cup sugar until fluffy. Gradually beat in sweetened condensed milk, then melted chips, until smooth. Add eggs and vanilla; beat well. Pour over crust.

3. Bake 60 to 70 minutes or until center is almost set. Remove from oven. With knife, loosen cake from side of pan. Cool. Remove side of pan. Refrigerate until cold. Garnish with Chocolate Drizzle, whipped topping and Mini Kisses™. Store, covered, in refrigerator.
Makes 12 servings

Chocolate Drizzle: Melt 2 tablespoons butter in small saucepan over low heat; add 2 tablespoons HERSHEY®S Cocoa and 2 tablespoons water. Cook and stir until slightly thickened. Do not boil. Cool slightly. Gradually add 1 cup powdered sugar and ½ teaspoon vanilla extract, beating with whisk until smooth. Makes about ¾ cup.

Tip: If desired, spoon drizzle into small heavy seal-top plastic bag. With scissors, make small diagonal cut in bottom corner of bag. Squeeze drizzle over top of cake.

Chocolate Spice Cake

1¾ cups all-purpose flour
1¼ cups sugar
⅓ cup HERSHEY®S Cocoa
2 teaspoons baking soda
1 teaspoon ground cinnamon
½ teaspoon ground nutmeg
¼ teaspoon ground allspice
⅛ teaspoon salt
1½ cups applesauce
½ cup milk
½ cup (1 stick) butter or margarine, melted
1 teaspoon vanilla extract
1 cup chopped nuts (optional)
½ cup raisins
Vanilla Glaze (recipe follows)

1. Heat oven to 350°F. Grease and flour 13×9×2-inch baking pan.

2. Stir together flour, sugar, cocoa, baking soda, cinnamon, nutmeg, allspice and salt in large bowl. Stir in applesauce, milk, butter and vanilla; beat until well blended. Add nuts, if desired, and raisins. Pour batter evenly into prepared pan.

3. Bake 40 to 45 minutes or until wooden pick inserted in center comes out clean. Cool completely in pan on wire rack. Drizzle with Vanilla Glaze.   *Makes 12 to 15 servings*

Vanilla Glaze: Combine 1¼ cups powdered sugar, 2 tablespoons softened butter or margarine, 1 to 2 tablespoons hot water or milk and ½ teaspoon vanilla extract in medium bowl; beat with whisk until smooth and of desired consistency. Makes about ¾ cup glaze.

Reese's® Chocolate Peanut Butter Cheesecake

Sweet Potato Pecan Pie

Prep Time: 30 minutes
Bake Time: 45 minutes

  1 pound sweet potatoes or yams, cooked and peeled
  ¼ cup (½ stick) butter or margarine, softened
  1 (14-ounce) can EAGLE BRAND® Sweetened Condensed Milk (NOT evaporated
    milk)
  1 egg
  1 teaspoon grated orange peel
  1 teaspoon ground cinnamon
  1 teaspoon vanilla extract
  ½ teaspoon ground nutmeg
  ¼ teaspoon salt
  1 (6-ounce) graham cracker crumb pie crust
    Pecan Topping (recipe follows)

1. Preheat oven to 425°F. In large mixing bowl, beat hot sweet potatoes and butter until smooth. Add Eagle Brand and remaining ingredients except crust and Pecan Topping; mix well. Pour into crust.

2. Bake 20 minutes. Meanwhile, prepare Pecan Topping.

3. Remove pie from oven; *reduce oven temperature to 350°F.* Spoon Pecan Topping over pie.

4. Bake 25 minutes longer or until set. Cool. Serve warm or at room temperature. Garnish with orange zest twist, if desired. Refrigerate leftovers.   *Makes 1 pie*

Pecan Topping: In small mixing bowl, beat 1 egg, 2 tablespoons firmly packed light brown sugar, 2 tablespoons dark corn syrup, 1 tablespoon melted butter and ½ teaspoon maple flavoring. Stir in 1 cup chopped pecans.

Sweet Potato Pecan Pie

Country Peach Tart

Pastry for single-crust 9-inch pie
4 cups sliced, pitted, peeled fresh
    peaches or frozen peaches, thawed
½ cup EQUAL® SPOONFUL*
1 tablespoon all-purpose flour
½ teaspoon ground cinnamon
¼ teaspoon almond extract

*May substitute 12 packets Equal® sweetener.

• Roll pastry on floured surface to 12-inch circle; transfer to ungreased baking sheet. Combine peaches, Equal®, flour, cinnamon and almond extract; toss gently until peaches are evenly coated with mixture.

• Arrange peach mixture over pastry, leaving 2-inch border around edge of pastry. Bring edge of pastry toward center, overlapping as necessary.

• Bake tart in preheated 425°F oven 25 to 30 minutes or until crust is golden brown and peaches are tender. Serve warm or at room temperature.   *Makes 8 servings*

Candy Bar Pie

Prep Time: 15 minutes
Chilling Time: 4 hours

    4 ounces cream cheese, softened
1¾ cups plus 1 tablespoon cold milk,
        divided
    1 (12-ounce) tub COOL WHIP®
        Whipped Topping, thawed, divided
    2 packages (2.07 ounces each)
        chocolate-covered caramel peanut
        nougat bars, chopped
    1 (4-serving size) package JELL-O®
        Chocolate Flavor Instant Pudding
        & Pie Filling
    1 (6-ounce) READY CRUST® Chocolate
        Pie Crust

1. Mix cream cheese and 1 tablespoon milk in medium bowl with wire whisk until smooth. Gently stir in 2 cups whipped topping and chopped candy bars; set aside.

2. Pour remaining 1¾ cups milk into another medium bowl. Add pudding mix. Beat with wire whisk 1 minute. Gently stir in ½ cup whipped topping. Spread half of pudding mixture on bottom of crust. Spread cream cheese mixture over pudding mixture. Top with remaining pudding mixture.

3. Refrigerate 4 hours or until set. Garnish with remaining whipped topping. Refrigerate leftovers.   *Makes 8 servings*

Caramel-Pecan Pie

    3 eggs
⅔ cup sugar
    1 cup (12-ounce jar) SMUCKER'S®
        Caramel Topping
    ¼ cup butter or margarine, melted
1½ cups pecan halves
    1 (9-inch) unbaked pie shell

In mixing bowl, beat eggs slightly with fork. Add sugar, stirring until dissolved. Stir in topping and butter; mix well. Stir in pecan halves. Pour filling into pie shell.

Bake at 350°F for 45 minutes or until knife inserted near center comes out clean. Cool completely on rack before serving. Cover and store in refrigerator.   *Makes 6 to 8 servings*

Country Peach Tart

Chocolate Fudge Pie

Prep Time: about 30 minutes
Bake Time: about 40 minutes

Crust
    1 unbaked Classic CRISCO® Single
        Crust (recipe follows)

Filling
    ¼ CRISCO® Stick or ¼ cup CRISCO®
        all-vegetable shortening
    1 bar (4 ounces) sweet baking chocolate
    1 can (14 ounces) sweetened condensed
        milk
    ½ cup all-purpose flour
    2 eggs, beaten
    1 teaspoon vanilla
    ¼ teaspoon salt
    1 cup flake coconut
    1 cup chopped pecans

Garnish
    **Unsweetened whipped cream or ice
        cream**

1. For crust, prepare as directed. Do not bake. Heat oven to 350°F. Place wire rack on countertop for cooling pie.

2. For filling, melt ¼ cup shortening and chocolate in heavy saucepan over low heat. Remove from heat. Stir in sweetened condensed milk, flour, eggs, vanilla and salt; mix well. Stir in coconut and nuts. Pour into unbaked pie crust.

3. Bake at 350°F for 40 minutes or until toothpick inserted into center comes out clean. Cool completely on wire rack.

4. Serve with unsweetened whipped cream or ice cream, if desired. Refrigerate leftover pie.

Makes 1 (9-inch) pie (8 servings)

Classic Crisco® Single Crust

    1⅓ cups all-purpose flour
    ½ teaspoon salt
    ½ CRISCO® Stick or ½ cup CRISCO®
        all-vegetable shortening
    3 tablespoons cold water

1. Spoon flour into measuring cup and level. Combine flour and salt in medium bowl.

2. Cut in ½ cup shortening using pastry blender or 2 knives until all flour is blended to form pea-size chunks.

3. Sprinkle with water, 1 tablespoon at a time. Toss lightly with fork until dough forms a ball.

4. Press dough between hands to form 5- to 6-inch "pancake." Flour rolling surface and rolling pin lightly. Roll dough into circle. Trim circle 1 inch larger than upside-down pie plate. Carefully remove trimmed dough. Set aside to reroll and use for pastry cutout garnish, if desired.

5. Fold dough into quarters. Unfold and press into pie plate. Fold edge under. Flute.

6. **For recipes using a baked pie crust,** heat oven to 425°F. Prick bottom and side thoroughly with fork (50 times) to prevent shrinkage. Bake at 425°F for 10 to 15 minutes or until lightly browned.

7. **For recipes using an unbaked pie crust,** follow directions given for that recipe.

Makes 1 (9-inch) single crust

Chocolate Fudge Pie

Chocolate Truffle Tart

Crust
- ⅔ cup all-purpose flour
- ½ cup powdered sugar
- ½ cup ground walnuts
- 6 tablespoons butter or margarine, softened
- ⅓ cup NESTLÉ® TOLL HOUSE® Baking Cocoa

Filling
- 1¼ cups heavy whipping cream
- ¼ cup granulated sugar
- 2 cups (12-ounce package) NESTLÉ® TOLL HOUSE® Semi-Sweet Chocolate Morsels
- 2 tablespoons seedless raspberry jam
  Sweetened whipped cream (optional)
  Fresh raspberries (optional)

For Crust
PREHEAT oven to 350°F.

BEAT flour, powdered sugar, nuts, butter and cocoa in large mixer bowl until soft dough forms. Press dough onto bottom and up side of ungreased 9- or 9½-inch fluted tart pan with removable bottom or 9-inch pie plate.

BAKE for 12 to 14 minutes or until puffed. Cool completely in pan on wire rack.

For Filling
BRING cream and granulated sugar in medium saucepan *just to a boil,* stirring occasionally. Remove from heat. Stir in morsels and jam; let stand for 5 minutes. Whisk until smooth. Transfer to small mixer bowl. Cover; refrigerate for 45 to 60 minutes or until mixture is cooled and slightly thickened.

BEAT for 20 to 30 seconds or just until color lightens slightly. Spoon into crust. Refrigerate until firm. Remove side of pan; garnish with whipped cream and raspberries.
Makes 8 servings

Coconut Peach Crunch Pie

Prep Time: 15 minutes
Baking Time: 35 to 40 minutes

- 1 (6-ounce) READY CRUST® Shortbread Pie Crust
- 1 egg yolk, beaten
- 1 (21-ounce) can peach pie filling
- 1 cup flaked coconut
- ½ cup all-purpose flour
- ½ cup sugar
- ¼ cup wheat germ
- ¼ cup margarine, melted

1. Preheat oven to 375°F. Brush bottom and sides of crust with egg yolk; bake on baking sheet 5 minutes or until golden brown.

2. Spoon peach filling into crust. Combine coconut, flour, sugar, wheat germ and margarine in small bowl. Mix until well blended. Spread over peach filling.

3. Bake on baking sheet 30 to 35 minutes or until filling is bubbly and topping is light brown. Cool on wire rack.   *Makes 8 servings*

Heavenly Chocolate Mousse Pie

Prep Time: 20 minutes
Chill Time: 15 minutes

- 4 (1-ounce) squares unsweetened chocolate, melted
- 1 (14-ounce) can EAGLE BRAND® Sweetened Condensed Milk (NOT evaporated milk)
- 1½ teaspoons vanilla extract
- 1 cup (½ pint) whipping cream, whipped
- 1 (6-ounce) chocolate crumb pie crust

1. In medium mixing bowl, beat melted chocolate with Eagle Brand and vanilla until well blended.

2. Chill 15 minutes or until cooled; stir until smooth. Fold in whipped cream.

3. Pour into crust. Chill thoroughly. Garnish as desired. Refrigerate leftovers.   *Makes 1 pie*

Chocolate Truffle Tart

Chocolate & Vanilla Swirl Tart

Tart Shell (recipe follows)
⅔ cup HERSHEY'S Semi-Sweet
   Chocolate Chips
½ cup milk, divided
2 tablespoons sugar
½ teaspoon unflavored gelatin
1 tablespoon cold water
⅔ cup HERSHEY'S Premier White
   Chips
1 teaspoon vanilla extract
1 cup (½ pint) cold whipping cream

1. Prepare Tart Shell.

2. Place chocolate chips, ¼ cup milk and sugar in small microwave-safe bowl. Microwave at HIGH (100%) 1 minute; stir. If necessary, microwave at HIGH an additional 15 seconds at a time, stirring after each heating, just until chips are melted when stirred. Cool about 20 minutes.

3. Sprinkle gelatin over water in small cup; let stand 2 minutes to soften. Place white chips and remaining ¼ cup milk in second small microwave-safe bowl. Microwave at HIGH 1 minute; stir. Add gelatin mixture and vanilla; stir until gelatin is dissolved. Cool about 20 minutes.

4. Beat whipping cream in small bowl on high speed of mixer until stiff; fold 1 cup whipped cream into vanilla mixture. Fold remaining whipped cream into chocolate mixture. Alternately, spoon chocolate and vanilla mixtures into prepared tart shell; swirl with knife for marbled effect. Refrigerate until firm. Cover; refrigerate leftover tart.
Makes 8 to 10 servings

Tart Shell

½ cup (1 stick) butter (do *not* use
   margarine), softened
2 tablespoons sugar
2 egg yolks
1 cup all-purpose flour

1. Heat oven to 375°F. Grease bottom and sides of fluted 8- or 9-inch tart pan.

2. Beat butter and sugar in small bowl until blended. Add egg yolks; mix well. Stir in flour until mixture is crumbly. Press onto bottom and up sides of prepared pan. (If dough is sticky, sprinkle with 1 tablespoon flour.) Prick bottom with fork to prevent puffing.

3. Bake 8 to 10 minutes or until lightly browned. Cool completely.

Orange Pecan Pie

3 eggs
½ cup GRANDMA'S® Molasses
½ cup light corn syrup
¼ cup orange juice
1 teaspoon grated orange peel
1 teaspoon vanilla
1½ cups whole pecan halves
1 (9-inch) unbaked pie shell
   Whipped cream (optional)

Heat oven to 350°F. In large bowl, beat eggs. Add molasses, corn syrup, orange juice, orange peel and vanilla; beat until well blended. Stir in pecans. Pour into unbaked pie shell. Bake 30 to 45 minutes or until filling sets. Cool on wire rack. Garnish as desired. Serve with whipped cream, if desired.
Makes 8 servings

Orange Pecan Pie

Best-Ever Apple Pie

2⅓ cups all-purpose flour, divided
¾ cup plus 1 tablespoon sugar, divided
½ teaspoon baking powder
½ teaspoon salt
¾ cup plus 3 tablespoons cold unsalted butter, cut into small pieces, divided
4 to 5 tablespoons ice water
1 egg, separated
7 medium Jonathan or Granny Smith apples, peeled, cored and sliced
1 tablespoon lemon juice
1¼ teaspoons ground cinnamon
1 tablespoon sour cream

1. Combine 2 cups flour, 1 tablespoon sugar, baking powder and salt in large bowl until well blended. Cut in ¾ cup butter using pastry blender or 2 knives until mixture resembles coarse crumbs. Add water, 1 tablespoon at a time, to flour mixture. Toss with fork until mixture holds together. Form dough into 2 discs. Wrap discs in plastic wrap; refrigerate 30 minutes or until firm.

2. Working with 1 disc at a time, roll out dough on lightly floured surface with lightly floured rolling pin into 12-inch circle, ⅛ inch thick. Ease dough into 9-inch glass pie plate. *Do not stretch dough.* Trim dough leaving ½-inch overhang; brush with egg white. Set aside.

3. Preheat oven to 450°F. Place apple slices in large bowl; sprinkle with lemon juice. Combine remaining ⅓ cup flour, ¾ cup sugar and cinnamon in small bowl until well blended. Add to apple mixture; toss to coat apples evenly. Spoon filling into prepared pie crust; place remaining 3 tablespoons butter on top of filling.

4. Moisten edge of dough with water. Roll out remaining disc. Place onto filled pie. Trim dough leaving ½-inch overhang.

5. Flute edge. Cut slits in dough at ½-inch intervals around edge to form flaps. Press 1 flap in toward center of pie and the next out toward rim of pie plate. Continue around edge. Cut 4 small slits in top of dough to allow steam to escape.

6. Combine egg yolk and sour cream in small bowl until well blended. Cover; refrigerate until ready to use.

7. Bake 10 minutes; *reduce oven temperature to 375°F.* Bake 35 minutes. Brush egg yolk mixture evenly on pie crust with pastry brush. Bake 20 to 25 minutes or until crust is deep golden brown. Cool completely on wire rack. Store loosely covered at room temperature 1 day or refrigerate up to 4 days.

Makes one (9-inch) pie

Peanut Butter Magic Pie

Prep Time: 15 minutes
Chilling Time: 4 hours

1 (8-ounce) package cream cheese, softened
¾ cup honey
1 (16-ounce) jar creamy or chunky peanut butter
1 (8-ounce) tub frozen non-dairy whipped topping, thawed
1 (6-ounce) READY CRUST® Chocolate Pie Crust
2 (1-ounce) squares semi-sweet baking chocolate
½ teaspoon shortening

1. Beat cream cheese and honey in medium bowl until well combined. Stir in peanut butter; mix well. Fold in whipped topping. Spoon into crust.

2. Heat chocolate and shortening in small saucepan over low heat until melted; drizzle over pie.

3. Chill 4 hours or overnight. Refrigerate leftovers.

Makes 8 servings

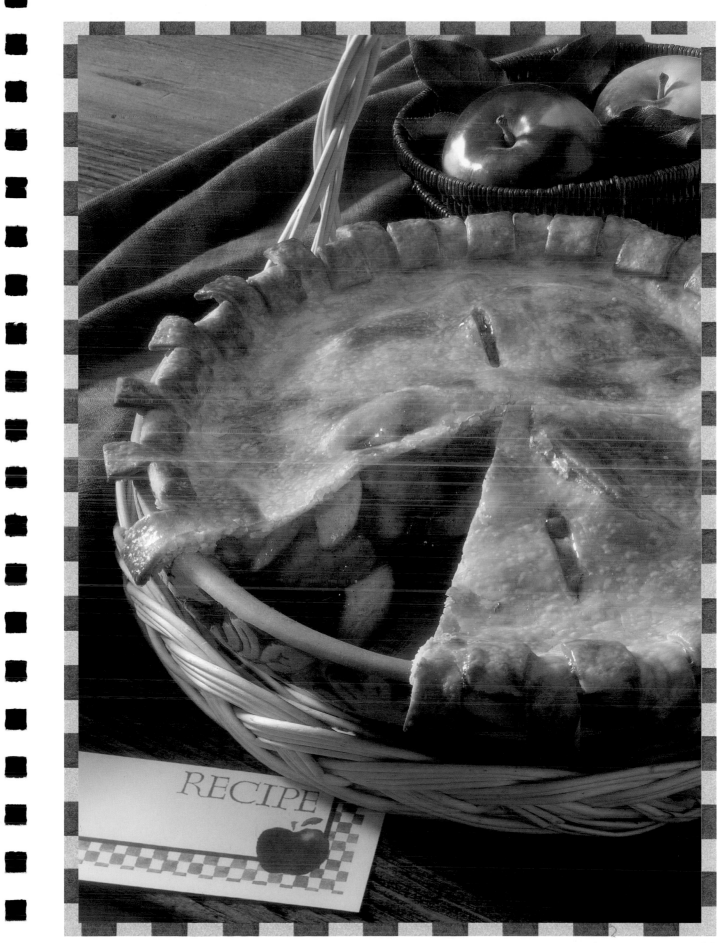

Nestlé® Toll House® Chocolate Chip Pie

1 *unbaked* 9-inch (4-cup volume)
    deep-dish pie shell*
2 eggs
½ cup all-purpose flour
½ cup granulated sugar
½ cup packed brown sugar
¾ cup (1½ sticks) butter, softened
1 cup (6 ounces) NESTLÉ® TOLL
    HOUSE® Semi-Sweet Chocolate
    Morsels
1 cup chopped nuts
    Sweetened whipped cream or ice
    cream (optional)

*If using frozen pie shell, use deep-dish style, thawed
completely. Bake on baking sheet; increase baking time
slightly.*

PREHEAT oven to 325°F.

BEAT eggs in large mixer bowl on high speed
until foamy. Beat in flour, granulated sugar and
brown sugar. Beat in butter. Stir in morsels and
nuts. Spoon into pie shell.

BAKE for 55 to 60 minutes or until knife
inserted halfway between outside edge and
center comes out clean. Cool on wire rack.
Serve warm with whipped cream.

Makes 8 servings

Wisconsin Ricotta Tart with Kiwi and Raspberry Sauce

⅓ cup all-purpose flour
⅓ cup packed brown sugar
3 tablespoons butter
1 cup flaked coconut
½ cup chopped pecans or macadamia
    nuts
2 cups (16 ounces) Wisconsin Ricotta
    cheese
½ cup powdered sugar
1 teaspoon grated lime peel
1 teaspoon vanilla
1 package (10 ounces) frozen
    raspberries, thawed
1 kiwifruit

Preheat oven to 350°F. Combine flour and
brown sugar; cut in butter until mixture
resembles coarse crumbs. Stir in coconut and
nuts. Press into 10-inch tart pan or pie plate.
Bake crust 15 minutes. Remove from oven and
cool.

Combine cheese, powdered sugar, lime peel and
vanilla in food processor or blender; process
until smooth. Spoon mixture into prepared
crust. Refrigerate 1 hour. Before serving, place
raspberries in food processor or blender; process
until sauce forms. Cut kiwi into slices and
arrange in circle on top of tart.* Drizzle tart
with ½ of the raspberry sauce. Serve with
remaining sauce.   *Makes 8 to 10 servings*

*Recipe can be prepared to this point and refrigerated
until ready to serve.*

Favorite recipe from **Wisconsin Milk
Marketing Board**

Nestlé® Toll House® Chocolate Chip Pie

Pineapple Fruit Tart

¼ cup ground almonds (about
    2 tablespoons whole almonds)
¼ cup butter or margarine, softened
¼ cup sugar
2 tablespoons milk
½ teaspoon almond extract
¾ cup all-purpose flour
2 packages (3 ounces each) cream
    cheese, softened
2 tablespoons sour cream
¼ cup apricot preserves, divided
1 teaspoon vanilla extract
1 can (15¼ ounces) DEL MONTE®
    Sliced Pineapple In Its Own Juice,
    drained and cut in halves
2 kiwifruits, peeled, sliced and cut into
    halves
1 cup sliced strawberries

1. Combine almonds, butter, sugar, milk and almond extract; mix well. Blend in flour. Chill dough 1 hour.

2. Press dough evenly onto bottom and up side of tart pan with removable bottom.

3. Bake at 350°F, 15 to 18 minutes or until golden brown. Cool.

4. Combine cream cheese, sour cream, 1 tablespoon apricot preserves and vanilla. Spread onto crust. Arrange pineapple, kiwi and strawberries over cream cheese mixture.

5. Heat remaining 3 tablespoons apricot preserves in small saucepan over low heat. Spoon over fruit. *Makes 8 servings*

Nectarine Pecan Tart

Pecan Crust
1 cup wafer crumbs
½ cup pecan pieces
2 tablespoons sugar
3 tablespoons unsalted butter, melted

Cream Cheese Filling
1 package (8 ounces) plus 1 package
    (3 ounces) cream cheese, softened
3 tablespoons sugar
2 tablespoons orange juice
½ teaspoon vanilla

Fruit Topping
2 ripe nectarines
4 tablespoons apricot jelly

1. For crust, preheat oven to 350°F. Place wafer crumbs, pecans and sugar in food processor; process until coarse crumbs form. Transfer to small bowl; stir in butter. Press crumb mixture onto bottom and partially up sides of 8-inch springform pan.

2. Bake 15 minutes or until lightly browned. Cool completely on wire rack.

3. For filling, beat cream cheese, sugar, juice and vanilla in medium bowl with electric mixer at low speed until blended. Increase speed to high, beat 2 minutes or until fluffy.

4. Pour filling into cooled crust, spreading mixture evenly to sides. Cover; refrigerate 3 hours or until set.

5. For topping, 30 minutes before serving, halve and slice nectarines. Arrange nectarines over cream cheese.

6. Melt jelly in small saucepan, whisking constantly, over low heat. Cool 1 minute. Drizzle jelly over nectarines. Refrigerate, uncovered, 20 minutes or until set.
Makes 6 servings

Note: For best results, serve tart same day as assembled.

Pineapple Fruit Tart

Easy Peanut Butter Chip Pie

1 package (3 ounces) cream cheese,
   softened
1 teaspoon lemon juice
1⅔ cups (10-ounce package) REESE'S®
   Peanut Butter Chips, divided
⅔ cup sweetened condensed milk (not
   evaporated milk)
1 cup (½ pint) cold whipping cream,
   divided
1 packaged chocolate or graham
   cracker crumb crust (6 ounces)
1 tablespoon powdered sugar
1 teaspoon vanilla extract

1. Beat cream cheese and lemon juice in
medium bowl until fluffy, about 2 minutes;
set aside.

2. Place 1 cup peanut butter chips and
sweetened condensed milk in medium
microwave-safe bowl. Microwave at HIGH
(100%) 45 seconds; stir. If necessary, microwave
an additional 15 seconds at a time, stirring
after each heating, until chips are melted and
mixture is smooth when stirred.

3. Add warm peanut butter mixture to cream
cheese mixture. Beat on medium speed until
blended, about 1 minute. Beat ½ cup whipping
cream in small bowl until stiff; fold into
peanut butter mixture. Pour into crust. Cover;
refrigerate several hours or overnight until firm.

4. Just before serving, combine remaining
½ cup whipping cream, powdered sugar and
vanilla in small bowl. Beat until stiff; spread
over filling. Garnish with remaining peanut
butter chips. Cover; refrigerate leftover pie.

Makes 6 to 8 servings

White Chocolate Cranberry Tart

1 refrigerated pie crust (half of
   15-ounce package)
1 cup sugar
2 eggs
¼ cup butter, melted
2 teaspoons vanilla
½ cup all-purpose flour
1 package (6 ounces) white chocolate
   baking bar, chopped
½ cup chopped macadamia nuts, lightly
   toasted*
½ cup dried cranberries, coarsely
   chopped

*Toast chopped macadamia nuts in hot skillet over
medium heat about 3 minutes or until fragrant.*

1. Preheat oven to 350°F. Place pie crust in
9-inch tart pan with removable bottom or pie
pan.

2. Combine sugar, eggs, butter and vanilla in
large bowl; mix well. Stir in flour until well
blended. Add white chocolate, nuts and
cranberries.

3. Pour filling into unbaked crust. Bake 50 to
55 minutes or until top of tart is crusty and
deep golden brown and knife inserted into
center comes out clean.

4. Cool completely on wire rack. Cover and
store at room temperature until serving time.

Makes 8 servings

Serving Suggestion: Top each serving with a
dollop of whipped cream flavored with ground
cinnamon, a favorite liqueur and grated orange
peel.

Easy Peanut Butter Chip Pie

Honey Strawberry Tart

⅓ cup honey
1 tablespoon lemon juice
1 baked or ready-to-eat 9-inch pie shell
4 cups halved fresh strawberries
Mint sprigs for garnish (optional)

Combine honey and lemon juice in small bowl; mix well. Brush bottom of pie shell with mixture. Fill shell with strawberries. Drizzle remaining honey mixture over berries. Garnish with mint sprigs, if desired.

Makes 8 servings

Tip: Prepare honey glaze and strawberries. Fill shell and glaze strawberries just before serving to prevent shell from becoming soggy.

Favorite recipe from **National Honey Board**

Quick & Easy Chocolate Chip Cherry Pie

1 can (21 ounces) cherry pie filling
1 tablespoon cornstarch
1 extra serving-size packaged graham cracker crumb crust (9 ounces)
1 package (8 ounces) cream cheese, softened
¼ cup sugar
2 eggs
½ teaspoon vanilla extract
½ teaspoon almond extract
½ cup HERSHEY'S Semi-Sweet Chocolate Chips *or* HERSHEY'S MINI CHIPS™ Semi-Sweet Chocolate Chips

1. Heat oven to 350°F.

2. Stir together pie filling and cornstarch in medium bowl until blended; pour into crust. Beat cream cheese, sugar, eggs, vanilla and almond extract in small bowl until blended; pour over pie filling. Sprinkle chocolate chips evenly over top.

3. Bake 35 to 40 minutes or until almost set in center. Cool completely on wire rack. Refrigerate until firm. Cover; refrigerate leftover pie.

Makes 8 to 10 servings

Apple Custard Tart

1 folded refrigerated unbaked pastry crust (one-half of 15-ounce package)
1 (14-ounce) can EAGLE BRAND® Sweetened Condensed Milk (NOT evaporated milk)
1½ cups sour cream
¼ cup thawed frozen apple juice concentrate
1 egg
1½ teaspoons vanilla extract
¼ teaspoon ground cinnamon
Apple Cinnamon Glaze (recipe follows)
2 medium all-purpose apples, cored, pared and thinly sliced
1 tablespoon butter or margarine

1. Let refrigerated pastry crust stand at room temperature according to package directions. Preheat oven to 375°F. On floured surface, roll pastry crust from center to edge, forming circle about 13 inches in diameter. Ease pastry into 11-inch tart pan with removable bottom. Trim pastry even with rim of pan. Place pan on baking sheet. Bake crust 15 minutes or until lightly golden.

2. Meanwhile, in medium mixing bowl, beat Eagle Brand, sour cream, apple juice concentrate, egg, vanilla and cinnamon in small bowl until smooth. Pour into baked pie crust. Bake 25 minutes or until center appears set when shaken. Cool 1 hour on wire rack. Prepare Apple Cinnamon Glaze.

3. In large skillet, cook apples in butter until tender-crisp. Arrange apples on top of tart; drizzle with Apple Cinnamon Glaze. Chill in refrigerator at least 4 hours. Store leftovers loosely covered in refrigerator.

Makes 1 tart

Apple Cinnamon Glaze: In small saucepan, combine ⅓ cup thawed frozen apple juice concentrate, 1 teaspoon cornstarch and ½ teaspoon ground cinnamon. Mix well. Cook and stir over low heat until thick and bubbly.

Apple Custard Tart

Chocolate and Pear Tart

Chocolate Tart Crust (recipe follows)
2 tablespoons sugar
2 teaspoons cornstarch
⅛ teaspoon salt
1 cup milk
2 egg yolks, beaten
1 cup HERSHEY'S Semi-Sweet
   Chocolate Chips
3 large fresh pears, such as Bartlett or
   Anjou
Apricot Glaze (recipe follows)

1. Prepare Chocolate Tart Crust.

2. Combine sugar, cornstarch and salt in heavy medium saucepan; gradually stir in milk. Cook and stir over medium heat until thickened and bubbly. Cook and stir 2 minutes more. Remove from heat; gradually stir about half of hot filling into beaten egg yolks. Pour egg yolk mixture back into hot filling in saucepan; bring to a gentle boil. Cook and stir 2 minutes more. Remove from heat.

3. Immediately add chocolate chips, stirring until chips are melted and mixture is smooth. Pour into Chocolate Tart Crust. Refrigerate several hours or until firm.

4. Core and peel pears; cut into thin slices. Place in circular pattern on top of filling. Immediately prepare Apricot Glaze. Spoon over top of fruit, covering completely. Refrigerate several hours or until firm; remove rim of pan. Serve cold. Cover; refrigerate leftover tart.

Makes 12 servings

Chocolate Tart Crust: Heat oven to 325°F. Grease and flour 9-inch round tart pan with removable bottom. Stir together ¾ cup all-purpose flour, ¼ cup powdered sugar and 1 tablespoon HERSHEY'S Cocoa in medium bowl. Mix in 6 tablespoons cold butter or margarine at low speed of mixer until blended and smooth. Press evenly with fingers onto bottom and up side of prepared pan. Bake 10 to 15 minutes; cool.

Apricot Glaze

¾ teaspoon unflavored gelatin
2 teaspoons cold water
2¼ teaspoons cornstarch
½ cup apricot nectar
¼ cup sugar
1 teaspoon lemon juice

1. Sprinkle gelatin over cold water in small cup; let stand several minutes to soften.

2. Combine cornstarch, apricot nectar, sugar and lemon juice in small saucepan; cook over medium heat, stirring constantly, until mixture is thickened. Remove from heat; immediately add gelatin mixture. Stir until smooth.

Makes ½ cup glaze

Grasshopper Mint Pie

Prep Time: 15 minutes
Chilling Time: 3 hours

1 (8-ounce) package cream cheese,
   softened
⅓ cup sugar
1 (8-ounce) tub frozen whipped
   topping, thawed
1 cup chopped KEEBLER® Fudge
   Shoppe® Grasshopper Cookies
3 drops green food coloring
1 (6-ounce) READY CRUST® Chocolate
   Pie Crust
Additional KEEBLER® Fudge
   Shoppe® Grasshopper Cookies,
   halved, for garnish

1. Mix cream cheese and sugar with electric mixer until well blended. Fold in whipped topping, chopped cookies and green food coloring. Spoon into crust.

2. Refrigerate 3 hours or overnight.

3. Garnish with cookie halves. Refrigerate leftovers.

Makes 8 servings

Grasshopper Mint Pie

Pumpkin Cheesecake Tarts

⅔ cup (about 15) crushed gingersnap
cookies
2 tablespoons butter or margarine,
melted
1 package (8 ounces) cream cheese,
softened
1 cup LIBBY'S® 100% Pure Pumpkin
½ cup granulated sugar
1 teaspoon pumpkin pie spice
1 teaspoon vanilla extract
2 eggs
2 tablespoons sour cream (optional)
2 tablespoons NESTLÉ® TOLL
HOUSE® Semi-Sweet Chocolate
Morsels (optional)

PREHEAT oven to 325°F. Paper-line
12 muffin cups.

COMBINE cookie crumbs and butter in small
bowl. Press scant tablespoon onto bottom of
each prepared muffin cup. Bake for 5 minutes.

BEAT cream cheese, pumpkin, sugar, pumpkin
pie spice and vanilla extract in small mixer
bowl until blended. Add eggs; beat well. Pour
into muffin cups, filling ¾ full.

BAKE for 25 to 30 minutes. Cool in pan on
wire rack. Remove tarts from pan; refrigerate.
Garnish with sour cream. Place morsels in
heavy-duty resealable plastic food storage
bag. Microwave on HIGH (100%) power for
20 seconds; knead. Microwave at additional
10-second intervals, kneading until smooth.
Cut tiny corner from bag; squeeze to drizzle
over tarts.   *Makes 12 tarts*

Very Cherry Pie

4 cups frozen unsweetened tart
cherries
1 cup dried tart cherries
1 cup sugar
2 tablespoons quick-cooking tapioca
½ teaspoon almond extract
Pastry for double-crust 9-inch pie
¼ teaspoon ground nutmeg
1 tablespoon butter

Combine frozen cherries, dried cherries, sugar,
tapioca and almond extract in large mixing
bowl; mix well. (It is not necessary to thaw
cherries before using.) Let cherry mixture stand
15 minutes.

Line 9-inch pie plate with pastry; fill with
cherry mixture. Sprinkle with nutmeg. Dot
with butter. Cover with top crust, cutting slits
for steam to escape. Or, cut top crust into strips
for lattice top.

Bake in preheated 375°F oven about 1 hour or
until crust is golden brown and filling is bubbly.
If necessary, cover edge of crust with foil to
prevent overbrowning.   *Makes 8 servings*

Note: Two (16-ounce) cans unsweetened tart
cherries, well drained, can be substituted for
frozen tart cherries. Dried cherries are available
at gourmet and specialty food stores and at
selected supermarkets.

Favorite recipe from **Cherry Marketing
Institute**

Blueberry Crumble Pie

Prep Time: 15 minutes
Baking Time: 40 minutes

1 (6-ounce) READY CRUST® Graham
Cracker Pie Crust
1 egg yolk, beaten
1 (21-ounce) can blueberry pie filling
⅓ cup all-purpose flour
⅓ cup quick-cooking oats
¼ cup sugar
3 tablespoons margarine, melted

1. Preheat oven to 375°F. Brush bottom and
sides of crust with egg yolk; bake on baking
sheet 5 minutes or until light brown.

2. Pour blueberry pie filling into crust.
Combine flour, oats and sugar in small bowl;
mix in margarine. Spoon over pie filling.

3. Bake on baking sheet about 35 minutes or
until filling is bubbly and topping is browned.
Cool on wire rack.   *Makes 8 servings*

Very Cherry Pie

Decadent Brownie Pie

Prep Time: 25 minutes
Bake Time: 45 to 50 minutes

 1 (9-inch) unbaked pastry shell
 1 cup (6 ounces) semi-sweet chocolate
   chips
 ¼ cup (½ stick) butter or margarine
 1 (14-ounce) can EAGLE BRAND®
   Sweetened Condensed Milk
   (NOT evaporated milk)
 ½ cup biscuit baking mix
 2 eggs
 1 teaspoon vanilla extract
 1 cup chopped nuts
   Vanilla ice cream

1. Preheat oven to 375°F. Bake pastry shell
10 minutes; remove from oven. Reduce oven
temperature to 325°F.

2. In small saucepan over low heat, melt chips
with butter.

3. In large mixing bowl, beat chocolate
mixture with Eagle Brand, biscuit mix, eggs
and vanilla until smooth. Add nuts. Pour into
baked pastry shell.

4. Bake 35 to 40 minutes or until center is set.
Serve warm or at room temperature with ice
cream. Refrigerate leftovers.

Makes 1 (9-inch) pie

Rustic Apple Croustade

 1⅓ cups all-purpose flour
 ¼ teaspoon salt
 2 tablespoons butter or margarine
 2 tablespoons vegetable shortening
 4 to 5 tablespoons ice water
 ⅓ cup packed light brown sugar
 1 tablespoon cornstarch
 1 teaspoon cinnamon, divided
 3 large Jonathan or MacIntosh apples,
   peeled, cored and thinly sliced
   (4 cups)
 1 egg white, beaten
 1 tablespoon granulated sugar

1. Combine flour and salt in small bowl. Cut in
butter and shortening with pastry blender or
two knives until mixture resembles coarse
crumbs. Mix in ice water, 1 tablespoon at a
time, until mixture comes together and forms
a soft dough. Wrap in plastic wrap; refrigerate
30 minutes.

2. Preheat oven to 375°F. Roll out pastry on
floured surface to ⅛-inch thickness. Cut into
12-inch circle. Transfer pastry to nonstick
jelly-roll pan.

3. Combine brown sugar, cornstarch and
¾ teaspoon cinnamon in medium bowl; mix
well. Add apples; toss well. Spoon apple
mixture into center of pastry, leaving 1½-inch
border. Fold pastry over apples, folding edges
in gently and pressing down lightly. Brush
egg white over pastry. Combine remaining
¼ teaspoon cinnamon and granulated sugar
in small bowl; sprinkle evenly over tart.

4. Bake 35 to 40 minutes or until apples are
tender and crust is golden brown. Let stand
20 minutes before serving. Cut into wedges.

Makes 8 servings

Decadent Brownie Pie

Michigan Blueberry Pie

Crust
Classic CRISCO® Double Crust
(recipe follows)

Filling
3 packages (12 ounces each) frozen
  blueberries, thawed and drained,
  reserving liquid
¼ cup quick-cooking tapioca
1½ cups sugar
¼ cup cornstarch
2 tablespoons grated orange peel
1 tablespoon butter or margarine
1 tablespoon cinnamon

Glaze
Milk
Sugar (optional)

1. For crust, prepare as directed. Press bottom crust into 9-inch pie plate. Do not bake. Heat oven to 425°F.

2. For filling, pour reserved liquid into medium saucepan. Stir in tapioca. Let stand 5 minutes. Stir in 1½ cups sugar and cornstarch. Cook and stir on medium heat until mixture comes to a boil and thickens. Stir in orange peel, butter and cinnamon. Fold in blueberries. Bring to a boil. Pour into unbaked pie crust. Moisten pastry edge with water.

3. Roll top crust same as bottom. Lift onto filled pie. Trim ½ inch beyond edge of pie plate. Fold top edge under bottom crust. Flute.

4. For glaze, brush with milk. Sprinkle with sugar, if desired. Cut slits in top crust to allow steam to escape.

5. Bake at 425°F for 45 minutes, or until filling in center is bubbly and crust is golden brown. *Do not overbake.* Cover edge with foil, if necessary, to prevent overbrowning. Serve barely warm or at room temperature.

Makes 1 (9-inch) pie

Classic Crisco® Double Crust

2 cups all-purpose flour
1 teaspoon salt
¾ CRISCO® Stick or ¾ cup CRISCO®
  all-vegetable shortening
5 tablespoons cold water (or more as
  needed)

1. Spoon flour into measuring cup and level. Combine flour and salt in medium bowl.

2. Cut in ¾ cup shortening using pastry blender or 2 knives until all flour is blended to form pea-size chunks.

3. Sprinkle with water, 1 tablespoon at a time. Toss lightly with fork until dough forms a ball. Divide dough in half.

4. Press dough between hands to form two 5- to 6-inch "pancakes." Flour rolling surface and rolling pin lightly. Roll both halves of dough into circle. Trim one circle of dough 1 inch larger than upside-down pie plate. Carefully remove trimmed dough. Set aside to reroll and use for pastry cutout garnish, if desired.

5. Fold dough into quarters. Unfold and press into pie plate. Trim edge even with plate. Add desired filling to unbaked crust. Moisten pastry edge with water. Lift top crust onto filled pie. Trim ½ inch beyond edge of pie plate. Fold top edge under bottom crust. Flute. Cut slits in top crust to allow steam to escape. Follow baking directions given for that recipe.

Makes 1 (9-inch) double crust

Easy Breads

Contents

Classic Quick Breads

MINI PUMPKIN CRANBERRY BREADS
♥ ♥ ♥

      3 cups all-purpose flour
      1 tablespoon plus 2 teaspoons pumpkin pie spice
      2 teaspoons baking soda
   1½ teaspoons salt
      3 cups granulated sugar
      1 can (15 ounces) LIBBY'S® 100% Pure Pumpkin
      4 eggs
      1 cup vegetable oil
      ½ cup orange juice or water
      1 cup sweetened dried, fresh or frozen cranberries

PREHEAT oven to 350°F. Grease and flour five or six 5×3-inch mini disposable or meat loaf pans.

COMBINE flour, pumpkin pie spice, baking soda and salt in large bowl. Combine sugar, pumpkin, eggs, vegetable oil and orange juice in large mixer bowl; beat until just blended. Add pumpkin mixture to flour mixture; stir just until moistened. Fold in cranberries. Spoon batter into prepared loaf pans.

BAKE for 50 to 55 minutes or until wooden pick inserted in center comes out clean. Cool in pans on wire racks for 10 minutes; remove to wire racks to cool completely.

Makes 5 or 6 mini loaves

Mini Pumpkin Cranberry Bread

CHEDDAR-APPLE BREAD

♥ ♥ ♥

2 cups all-purpose flour
2 teaspoons baking powder
1 teaspoon baking soda
¼ teaspoon salt
1 cup packed light brown sugar
½ cup butter, softened
2 eggs
1 teaspoon vanilla
1 cup sour cream
¼ cup milk
1 cup (4 ounces) shredded Cheddar cheese
1½ cups diced dried apples

Preheat oven to 350°F. Spray 9×5-inch loaf pan with nonstick cooking spray; set aside.

Combine flour, baking powder, baking soda and salt in small bowl. Beat sugar and butter in large bowl with electric mixer at medium speed until light and fluffy. Beat in eggs and vanilla until blended. Add flour mixture to butter mixture alternately with sour cream and milk, beginning and ending with flour mixture. Beat after each addition. Stir in cheese and apples until blended. Spoon into prepared pan.

Bake 50 to 55 minutes or until toothpick inserted into center comes out clean. Cool in pan on wire rack 15 minutes. Remove from pan and cool completely on wire rack.

Makes 12 servings

Tip: If brown sugar becomes hard during storage, it can be difficult to measure. To soften, put it in a microwavable container and microwave at HIGH 30 to 60 seconds.

Cheddar-Apple Bread

ORANGE CINNAMON SWIRL BREAD

♥ ♥ ♥

BREAD
>   1 package DUNCAN HINES® Bakery-Style Cinnamon Swirl
>   Muffin Mix
>   1 egg
>   ⅔ cup orange juice
>   1 tablespoon grated orange peel

ORANGE GLAZE
>   ½ cup confectioners' sugar
>   2 to 3 teaspoons orange juice
>   1 teaspoon grated orange peel
>   Quartered orange slices for garnish (optional)

1. Preheat oven to 350°F. Grease and flour 8½×4½×2½-inch loaf pan.

2. For bread, combine muffin mix and contents of topping packet from mix in large bowl. Break up any lumps. Add egg, ⅔ cup orange juice and 1 tablespoon orange peel. Stir until moistened, about 50 strokes. Knead swirl packet from mix for 10 seconds before opening. Squeeze contents on top of batter. Swirl into batter with knife or spatula, folding from bottom of bowl to get an even swirl. *Do not completely mix in.* Pour into prepared pan. Bake at 350°F for 55 to 60 minutes or until toothpick inserted in center comes out clean. Cool in pan 10 minutes. Loosen loaf from pan. Invert onto cooling rack. Turn right side up. Cool completely.

3. For orange glaze, place confectioners' sugar in small bowl. Add orange juice, 1 teaspoon at a time, stirring until smooth and of desired consistency. Stir in 1 teaspoon orange peel. Drizzle over loaf. Garnish with orange slices, if desired.   *Makes 1 loaf (12 slices)*

Tip: If glaze becomes too thin, add more confectioners' sugar. If glaze is too thick, add more orange juice.

Orange Cinnamon Swirl Bread

PEANUT BUTTER CHOCOLATE CHIP LOAVES

♥ ♥ ♥

3 cups all-purpose flour
1½ teaspoons baking powder
1 teaspoon baking soda
1 teaspoon salt
1 cup creamy peanut butter
½ cup granulated sugar
½ cup packed light brown sugar
½ cup butter, softened
2 eggs
1½ cups buttermilk*
2 teaspoons vanilla
1 cup miniature semisweet chocolate chips

Soured fresh milk can be substituted for buttermilk. To sour milk, combine 4½ teaspoons lemon juice plus enough milk to equal 1½ cups. Stir; let stand 5 minutes before using.

Preheat oven to 350°F. Spray two 8½×4½-inch loaf pans with nonstick cooking spray; set aside.

Sift flour, baking powder, baking soda and salt into large bowl. Beat peanut butter, granulated sugar, brown sugar and butter in second large bowl with electric mixer at medium speed until light and fluffy. Beat in eggs, one at a time. Beat in buttermilk and vanilla. Gradually add flour mixture. Beat at low speed until blended. Stir in chocolate chips. Divide batter evenly between prepared pans.

Bake 45 minutes or until toothpicks inserted into centers come out clean. Cool in pans on wire racks 10 minutes. Remove from pans and cool completely on wire racks.

Makes 24 servings

Variation: Stir in ¾ cup chocolate chips before baking; sprinkle with remaining ¼ cup after baking.

Peanut Butter Chocolate Chip Loaf

IRISH SODA BREAD

♥ ♥ ♥

4 cups all-purpose flour
¼ cup sugar
1 tablespoon baking powder
1 teaspoon baking soda
1 teaspoon salt
1 tablespoon caraway seeds
⅓ cup vegetable shortening
1 cup raisins or currants
1 egg
1¾ cups buttermilk*

Soured fresh milk can be substituted for buttermilk. To sour milk, combine 2 tablespoons lemon juice plus enough milk to equal 1¾ cups. Stir; let stand 5 minutes before using.

1. Preheat oven to 350°F. Grease large baking sheet; set aside.

2. Sift flour, sugar, baking powder, baking soda and salt into large bowl. Stir in caraway seeds. Cut in shortening with pastry blender or 2 knives until mixture resembles coarse crumbs. Stir in raisins. Beat egg in medium bowl using fork. Add buttermilk; beat until well combined. Add buttermilk mixture to flour mixture; stir until mixture forms soft dough that clings together and forms a ball.

3. Turn dough out onto well-floured surface. Knead dough gently 10 to 12 times. Place dough on prepared baking sheet. Pat dough into 7-inch round. Score top of dough with tip of sharp knife, making an "X" about 4 inches long and ¼ inch deep.

4. Bake 55 to 60 minutes or until toothpick inserted into center comes out clean. Immediately remove from baking sheet; cool on wire rack.** Bread is best eaten the day it is made.   *Makes 12 servings*

**For a sweet crust, combine 1 tablespoon sugar and 1 tablespoon water in small bowl; brush over hot loaf.*

Irish Soda Bread

ALOHA BREAD

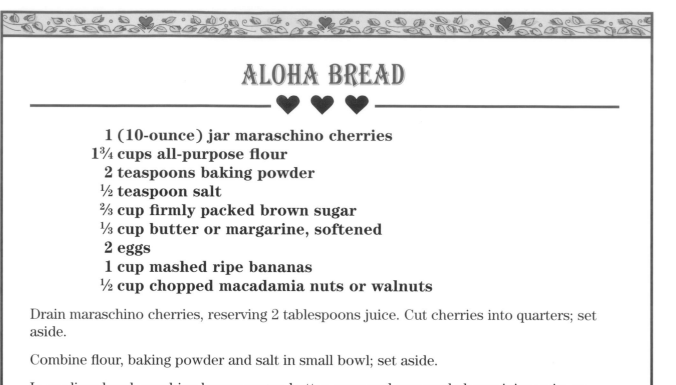

1 (10-ounce) jar maraschino cherries
1¾ cups all-purpose flour
2 teaspoons baking powder
½ teaspoon salt
⅔ cup firmly packed brown sugar
⅓ cup butter or margarine, softened
2 eggs
1 cup mashed ripe bananas
½ cup chopped macadamia nuts or walnuts

Drain maraschino cherries, reserving 2 tablespoons juice. Cut cherries into quarters; set aside.

Combine flour, baking powder and salt in small bowl; set aside.

In medium bowl, combine brown sugar, butter, eggs and reserved cherry juice; mix on medium speed of electric mixer until ingredients are thoroughly combined. Add flour mixture alternately with mashed bananas, beginning and ending with flour mixture. Stir in cherries and nuts. Lightly spray 9×5×3-inch loaf pan with nonstick cooking spray. Spread batter evenly in pan.

Bake in preheated 350°F oven 1 hour or until loaf is golden brown and wooden pick inserted near center comes out clean. Remove from pan and cool on wire rack. Store in tightly covered container or foil.   *Makes 1 loaf (about 16 slices)*

Favorite recipe from **Cherry Marketing Institute**

Aloha Bread

BLUEBERRY HILL BREAD

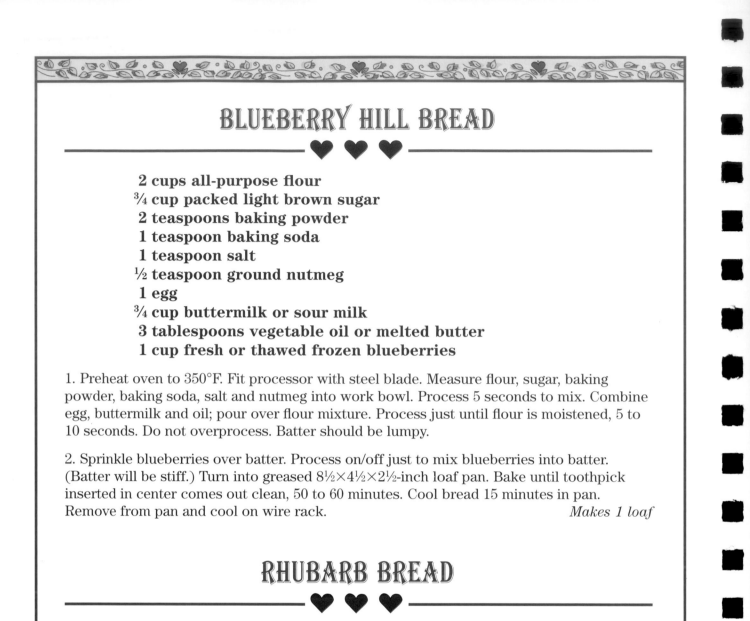

♥ ♥ ♥

2 cups all-purpose flour
¾ cup packed light brown sugar
2 teaspoons baking powder
1 teaspoon baking soda
1 teaspoon salt
½ teaspoon ground nutmeg
1 egg
¾ cup buttermilk or sour milk
3 tablespoons vegetable oil or melted butter
1 cup fresh or thawed frozen blueberries

1. Preheat oven to 350°F. Fit processor with steel blade. Measure flour, sugar, baking powder, baking soda, salt and nutmeg into work bowl. Process 5 seconds to mix. Combine egg, buttermilk and oil; pour over flour mixture. Process just until flour is moistened, 5 to 10 seconds. Do not overprocess. Batter should be lumpy.

2. Sprinkle blueberries over batter. Process on/off just to mix blueberries into batter. (Batter will be stiff.) Turn into greased 8½×4½×2½-inch loaf pan. Bake until toothpick inserted in center comes out clean, 50 to 60 minutes. Cool bread 15 minutes in pan. Remove from pan and cool on wire rack. *Makes 1 loaf*

RHUBARB BREAD

♥ ♥ ♥

Peel from ½ orange
1 cup sugar
¾ cup walnuts
¾ pound fresh rhubarb, cut into feed-tube lengths
2 cups all-purpose flour
1 tablespoon baking powder
1 teaspoon salt
1 teaspoon ground cinnamon
1 cup milk
2 eggs
⅓ cup butter, melted

1. Preheat oven to 350°F. Fit processor with steel blade. Process orange peel and sugar until peel is minced, about 1 minute; set aside. Process walnuts on/off to coarsely chop; set aside.

2. Fit processor with slicing blade. Process rhubarb until coarsely chopped; set aside.

3. Refit processor with steel blade. Add sugar mixture, rhubarb, walnuts, flour, baking powder, salt and cinnamon to work bowl. Process just until mixed, about 5 seconds. Add milk, eggs and butter. Process on/off just until flour is moistened. Do not overprocess. Batter should be lumpy.

4. Turn batter into greased 8½×4½×2½-inch loaf pan. Bake until toothpick inserted into center of loaf comes out clean, about 60 to 70 minutes. Cool bread 15 minutes in pan. Remove from pan and cool on wire rack.   *Makes 1 loaf*

ZUCCHINI NUT BREAD
♥ ♥ ♥

    2 eggs
    ½ **cup vegetable oil**
    1½ **cups all-purpose flour**
    1 cup chopped nuts *or* ½ **cup raisins and** ½ **cup chopped**
        nuts
    1 cup shredded zucchini
    ¾ **cup sugar**
    1½ **teaspoons ground cinnamon**
    1 teaspoon baking soda
    1 teaspoon vanilla
    ½ **teaspoon salt**
    ½ **teaspoon baking powder**

1. Preheat oven to 375°F. Fit processor with steel blade. Measure all ingredients into work bowl. Process just until flour is moistened, 5 to 10 seconds. Do not overprocess. Batter should be lumpy.

2. Pour batter into greased 8½×4½×2½-inch loaf pan or 2 greased 5¾×3¼×2-inch loaf pans. Bake until toothpick inserted into center comes out clean, about 1 hour for larger loaf or 30 to 35 minutes for smaller loaves. Cool bread 15 minutes in pan. Remove from pan and cool on wire rack.   *Makes 1 large or 2 small loaves*

GOLDEN APPLE BUTTERMILK BREAD

❤ ❤ ❤

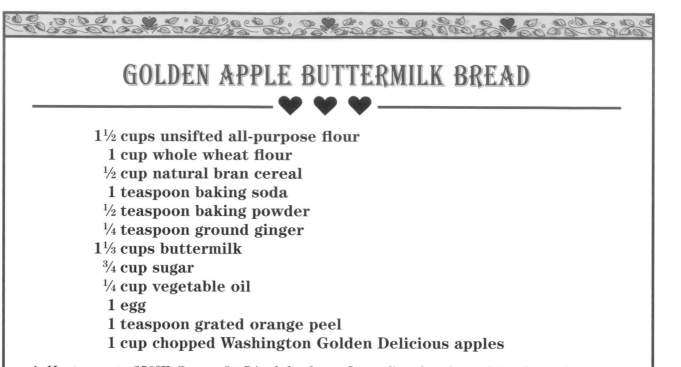

1½ cups unsifted all-purpose flour
1 cup whole wheat flour
½ cup natural bran cereal
1 teaspoon baking soda
½ teaspoon baking powder
¼ teaspoon ground ginger
1⅓ cups buttermilk
¾ cup sugar
¼ cup vegetable oil
1 egg
1 teaspoon grated orange peel
1 cup chopped Washington Golden Delicious apples

1. Heat oven to 350°F. Grease 9×5-inch loaf pan. In medium bowl, combine flours, bran cereal, baking soda, baking powder and ginger. In large bowl, beat together buttermilk, sugar, oil, egg and orange peel.

2. Add flour mixture to buttermilk mixture, stirring just until combined. Fold in apples. Spread batter in prepared pan and bake 45 to 50 minutes or until wooden toothpick inserted in center comes out clean. Cool bread in pan 10 minutes. Remove from pan and cool on wire rack.   *Makes 1 loaf (8 servings)*

Favorite recipe from **Washington Apple Commission**

Golden Apple Buttermilk Bread

PUMPKIN BREAD

❤ ❤ ❤

1 package (about 18 ounces) yellow cake mix
1 can (16 ounces) solid pack pumpkin
4 eggs
⅓ cup GRANDMA'S® Molasses
1 teaspoon cinnamon
1 teaspoon nutmeg
⅓ cup nuts, chopped (optional)
⅓ cup raisins (optional)

Preheat oven to 350°F. Grease two 9×5-inch loaf pans.

Combine all ingredients in large bowl and mix well. Beat at medium speed 2 minutes. Pour into prepared pans. Bake 60 minutes or until toothpick inserted into center comes out clean.

Makes 2 loaves

Hint: Serve with cream cheese or preserves, or top with cream cheese frosting or ice cream.

NUT AND RAISIN BREAD

❤ ❤ ❤

2 cups all-purpose flour
1½ cups bread flour
½ cup corn meal
½ cup brown sugar
4 teaspoons baking powder
1 teaspoon salt
1 cup chopped raisins
¾ cup chopped nuts
2 cups milk
½ cup GRANDMA'S® Molasses
¼ teaspoon baking soda

Heat oven to 375°F. In large bowl, sift and mix dry ingredients; add raisins and nuts. Add milk and mix well. In another bowl combine molasses and baking soda; add to flour mixture. Knead into a dough. Bake about 45 minutes or until golden brown.

Makes 8 servings

Pumpkin Bread

BANANA NUT BREAD

❤ ❤ ❤

½ cup granulated sugar
2 tablespoons brown sugar
5 tablespoons margarine
1⅓ cups mashed ripe bananas (2 medium)
1 egg
2 egg whites
2½ cups all-purpose flour
1 teaspoon baking soda
½ teaspoon salt
⅓ cup walnuts

Preheat oven to 375°F. Spray large loaf pan with nonstick cooking spray; set aside.

Beat sugars and margarine in large bowl with electric mixer until light and fluffy. Add bananas, egg and egg whites. Sift together flour, baking soda and salt in medium bowl; add to banana mixture. Stir in walnuts. Pour into prepared loaf pan.

Bake 1 hour or until wooden pick inserted in center comes out clean. Remove from pan. Cool on wire rack 10 minutes. Serve warm or cool completely.

Makes 1 loaf (16 servings)

Favorite recipe from **The Sugar Association, Inc.**

Banana Nut Bread

COCONUT CHOCOLATE CHIP LOAF

♥ ♥ ♥

**1 package DUNCAN HINES® Bakery-Style Chocolate Chip
Muffin Mix**
1⅓ cups toasted flaked coconut (see Tip)
¾ cup water
1 egg
½ teaspoon vanilla extract
Confectioners' sugar for garnish (optional)

1. Preheat oven to 350°F. Grease and flour 9×5×3-inch loaf pan.

2. Empty muffin mix into medium bowl. Break up any lumps. Add coconut, water, egg and vanilla extract. Stir until moistened, about 50 strokes. Pour into prepared pan. Bake at 350°F for 45 to 50 minutes or until toothpick inserted in center comes out clean. Cool in pan 15 minutes. Invert onto cooling rack. Turn right side up. Cool completely. Dust with confectioners' sugar, if desired.   *Makes 1 loaf (12 slices)*

Tip: Spread coconut evenly on baking sheet. Toast at 350°F for 5 minutes. Stir and toast 1 to 2 minutes longer or until light golden brown.

Coconut Chocolate Chip Loaf

APRICOT CARROT BREAD

♥ ♥ ♥

1¾ cups all-purpose flour
1 teaspoon baking powder
¼ teaspoon baking soda
¼ teaspoon salt
½ cup granulated sugar
½ cup finely shredded carrots
½ cup MOTT'S® Natural Apple Sauce
1 egg, beaten lightly
2 tablespoons vegetable oil
⅓ cup dried apricots, snipped into small bits
½ cup powdered sugar
2 teaspoons MOTT'S® Apple Juice

1. Preheat oven to 350°F. Spray 8×4-inch loaf pan with nonstick cooking spray.

2. In large bowl, combine flour, baking powder, baking soda and salt.

3. In small bowl, combine granulated sugar, carrots, apple sauce, egg and oil.

4. Stir apple sauce mixture into flour mixture just until moistened. (Batter will be thick.) Fold in apricots. Spread batter into prepared pan.

5. Bake 45 to 50 minutes or until toothpick inserted in center comes out clean. Cool in pan 10 minutes. Invert onto wire rack; turn right side up. Cool completely. For best flavor, wrap loaf in plastic wrap or foil; store at room temperature overnight.

6. Just before serving, in small bowl, combine powdered sugar and apple juice until smooth. Drizzle over top of loaf. Cut into 12 slices.   *Makes 12 servings*

Apricot Carrot Bread

WALNUT-CHOCOLATE QUICK BREAD

♥ ♥ ♥

1½ cups milk
1 cup sugar
⅓ cup vegetable oil
1 egg, beaten
1 tablespoon molasses
1 teaspoon vanilla
3 cups all-purpose flour
3 tablespoons unsweetened cocoa powder
2 teaspoons baking soda
2 teaspoons baking powder
1 teaspoon salt
1 cup chocolate chips
½ cup walnuts, coarsely chopped

1. Preheat oven to 350°F. Grease four 5×3-inch loaf pans; set aside.

2. Combine milk, sugar, oil, egg, molasses and vanilla in medium bowl. Stir until sugar is dissolved.

3. Whisk flour, cocoa, baking soda, baking powder and salt in large bowl. Add chocolate chips, nuts and sugar mixture; stir just until combined. Pour into prepared pans.

4. Bake 30 minutes or until toothpicks inserted into centers of loaves come out clean. Cool in pans 15 minutes. Remove from pans and cool on wire racks.   *Makes 4 loaves*

Muffin Variation: Preheat oven to 375°F. Spoon batter into 12 greased muffin cups. Bake 20 minutes or until toothpicks inserted into centers of muffins come out clean. Makes 12 muffins.

Walnut-Chocolate Quick Bread

MANGO BREAD

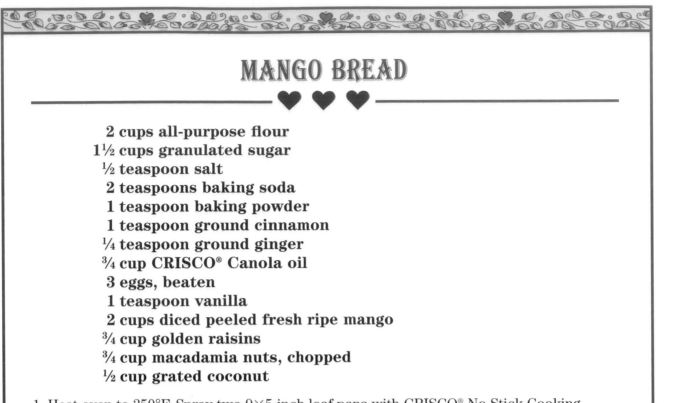

        2 cups all-purpose flour
    1½ cups granulated sugar
        ½ teaspoon salt
        2 teaspoons baking soda
        1 teaspoon baking powder
        1 teaspoon ground cinnamon
        ¼ teaspoon ground ginger
        ¾ cup CRISCO® Canola oil
        3 eggs, beaten
        1 teaspoon vanilla
        2 cups diced peeled fresh ripe mango
        ¾ cup golden raisins
        ¾ cup macadamia nuts, chopped
        ½ cup grated coconut

1. Heat oven to 350°F. Spray two 9×5-inch loaf pans with CRISCO® No-Stick Cooking Spray. Dust with flour; set aside.

2. Combine flour, sugar, salt, baking soda, baking powder, cinnamon and ginger in large bowl.

3. Combine oil, eggs and vanilla in medium bowl; mix well. Add to flour mixture; mix well. Fold in mango, raisins, nuts and coconut.

4. Pour batter into prepared loaf pans. Bake at 350°F for 45 to 60 minutes or until toothpick inserted in center of each loaf comes out clean and loaves are golden. Cool in pans 10 minutes. Turn out onto cooling rack; cool completely.

Makes 6 to 8 servings per loaf

Tip: A tradition in the Hawaiian Islands is to bring a loaf of bread to friends and neighbors when you are invited to their home. This bread is often given as a gift to new neighbors as a sign of welcome.

PINEAPPLE ALMOND DATE BREAD

♥ ♥ ♥

1 cup almonds, divided
2 cups all-purpose flour
1 teaspoon baking powder
1 teaspoon baking soda
¼ teaspoon ground nutmeg
¾ cup sugar
½ cup margarine, softened
1 egg
1 can (8 ounces) DOLE® Crushed Pineapple
  Grated peel from 1 orange (about 1 tablespoon)
1 cup DOLE® Chopped Dates

• Preheat oven to 350°F. Toast ¾ cup almonds; reserve remaining ¼ cup for topping.

• Combine flour, baking powder, baking soda and nutmeg in medium bowl.

• Beat sugar and margarine in large bowl until light and fluffy. Beat in egg until blended. Stir in undrained crushed pineapple and orange peel. Beat in flour mixture until blended. Stir in ¾ cup toasted almonds and dates.

• Turn batter into well-greased 9×5-inch loaf pan. Sprinkle remaining ¼ cup untoasted almonds on top. Bake 55 to 60 minutes or until toothpick inserted in center comes out clean. Cool in pan 10 minutes. Turn onto wire rack to cool completely.   *Makes 1 loaf*

Note: To toast almonds, spread in single layer on ungreased baking sheet. Bake in preheated 350°F oven 8 to 10 minutes or until lightly browned, stirring frequently. Let cool before using.

Old-Fashioned Muffins

BLUEBERRY WHITE CHIP MUFFINS

♥ ♥ ♥

2 cups all-purpose flour
½ cup granulated sugar
¼ cup packed brown sugar
2½ teaspoons baking powder
½ teaspoon salt
¾ cup milk
1 egg, lightly beaten
¼ cup butter or margarine, melted
½ teaspoon grated lemon peel
2 cups (12-ounce package) NESTLÉ® TOLL HOUSE®
   Premier White Morsels, *divided*
1½ cups fresh or frozen blueberries
   Streusel Topping (recipe follows)

PREHEAT oven to 375°F. Paper-line 18 muffin cups.

COMBINE flour, granulated sugar, brown sugar, baking powder and salt in large bowl. Stir in milk, egg, butter and lemon peel. Stir in *1½ cups* morsels and blueberries. Spoon into prepared muffin cups, filling almost full. Sprinkle with Streusel Topping.

BAKE for 22 to 25 minutes or until wooden pick inserted in center comes out clean. Cool in pans for 5 minutes; remove to wire racks to cool slightly.

PLACE *remaining* morsels in small, *heavy-duty* resealable plastic food storage bag. Microwave on MEDIUM-HIGH (70%) power for 30 seconds; knead. Microwave at additional 10- to 15-second intervals, kneading until smooth. Cut tiny corner from bag; squeeze to drizzle over muffins. Serve warm.   *Makes 18 muffins*

Streusel Topping: COMBINE ⅓ cup granulated sugar, ¼ cup all-purpose flour and ¼ teaspoon ground cinnamon in small bowl. Cut in 3 tablespoons butter or margarine with pastry blender or two knives until mixture resembles coarse crumbs.

Blueberry White Chip Muffins

PEACHY OAT BRAN MUFFINS

♥ ♥ ♥

1½ cups oat bran
½ cup all-purpose flour
⅓ cup firmly packed brown sugar
2 teaspoons baking powder
1 teaspoon cinnamon
½ teaspoon salt
¾ cup lowfat milk
1 egg, beaten
¼ cup vegetable oil
1 can (15 ounces) DEL MONTE® LITE® Yellow Cling Sliced
   Peaches, drained and chopped
⅓ cup chopped walnuts

1. Preheat oven to 425°F. Combine oat bran, flour, brown sugar, baking powder, cinnamon and salt; mix well.

2. Combine milk, egg and oil. Add to dry ingredients; stir just enough to blend. Fold in fruit and nuts.

3. Fill greased muffin cups with batter. Sprinkle with granulated sugar, if desired.

4. Bake 20 to 25 minutes or until golden brown.   *Makes 12 medium muffins*

Hint: Muffins can be frozen and reheated in microwave or toaster oven.

Prep Time: 10 minutes
Bake Time: 25 minutes

Peachy Oat Bran Muffins

CRANBERRY CHEESECAKE MUFFINS

♥ ♥ ♥

1 package (3 ounces) cream cheese, softened
4 tablespoons sugar, divided
1 cup reduced-fat (2%) milk
⅓ cup vegetable oil
1 egg
1 package (about 15 ounces) cranberry quick bread mix

1. Preheat oven to 400°F. Grease 12 muffin pan cups.

2. Beat cream cheese and 2 tablespoons sugar in small bowl until well blended.

3. Beat milk, oil and egg in large bowl until blended. Stir in quick bread mix just until dry ingredients are moistened.

4. Fill prepared muffin cups ¼ full with batter. Drop 1 teaspoon cream cheese mixture into center of each cup. Spoon remaining batter over cream cheese mixture.

5. Sprinkle batter with remaining 2 tablespoons sugar. Bake 17 to 22 minutes or until golden brown. Cool 5 minutes. Remove from muffin cups to wire rack to cool.

Makes 12 muffins

Prep and Bake Time: 30 minutes

Cranberry Cheesecake Muffins

PEANUT BUTTER MINI MUFFINS

♥ ♥ ♥

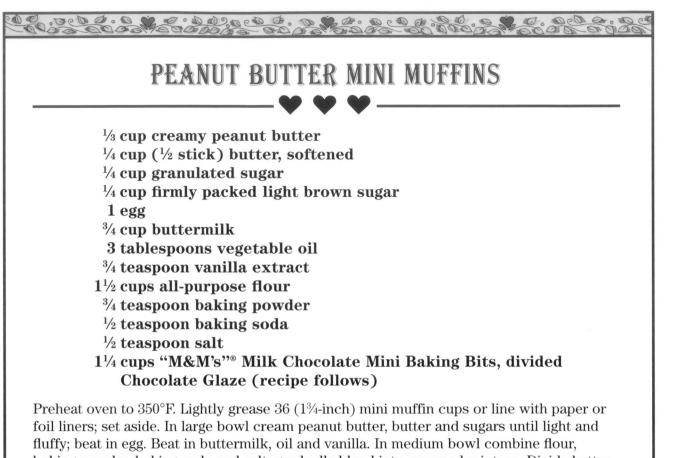

⅓ cup creamy peanut butter
¼ cup (½ stick) butter, softened
¼ cup granulated sugar
¼ cup firmly packed light brown sugar
1 egg
¾ cup buttermilk
3 tablespoons vegetable oil
¾ teaspoon vanilla extract
1½ cups all-purpose flour
¾ teaspoon baking powder
½ teaspoon baking soda
½ teaspoon salt
1¼ cups "M&M's"® Milk Chocolate Mini Baking Bits, divided
  Chocolate Glaze (recipe follows)

Preheat oven to 350°F. Lightly grease 36 (1¾-inch) mini muffin cups or line with paper or foil liners; set aside. In large bowl cream peanut butter, butter and sugars until light and fluffy; beat in egg. Beat in buttermilk, oil and vanilla. In medium bowl combine flour, baking powder, baking soda and salt; gradually blend into creamed mixture. Divide batter evenly among prepared muffin cups. Sprinkle batter evenly with ¾ cup "M&M's"® Milk Chocolate Mini Baking Bits. Bake 15 to 17 minutes or until toothpick inserted in centers comes out clean. Cool completely on wire racks. Prepare Chocolate Glaze. Place glaze in resealable plastic sandwich bag; seal bag. Cut tiny piece off one corner of bag (not more than ⅛ inch). Drizzle glaze over muffins. Decorate with remaining ½ cup "M&M's"® Milk Chocolate Mini Baking Bits; let glaze set. Store in tightly covered container.

Makes 3 dozen mini muffins

Chocolate Glaze: In top of double boiler over hot water melt 2 (1-ounce) squares semi-sweet chocolate and 1 tablespoon butter. Stir until smooth; let cool slightly.

Peanut Butter Mini Muffins

CHEDDAR AND APPLE MUFFINS

♥ ♥ ♥

2 cups buttermilk baking mix
½ to 1 teaspoon ground red pepper
½ teaspoon salt
⅔ cup milk
1 egg, lightly beaten
1 medium apple, peeled, cored and grated
1 cup (4 ounces) shredded sharp Cheddar cheese

1. Preheat oven to 375°F. Spray 12 (2½-inch) muffin pan cups with nonstick cooking spray.

2. Combine baking mix, red pepper and salt in large bowl. Add milk and egg; mix until just moistened. *Do not overmix.* Fold in apple and cheese.

3. Spoon batter into prepared muffin cups, filling ¾ full. Bake 20 to 25 minutes or until golden brown. Cool 5 minutes in pan. Loosen sides of muffins with knife; remove from pan to wire rack. Serve warm. *Makes 12 muffins*

Cheddar and Apple Muffins

CARROT AND RAISIN MUFFINS

♥ ♥ ♥

2 cups all-purpose flour
1 tablespoon baking powder
½ teaspoon ground allspice (optional)
¼ teaspoon salt
¾ cup firmly packed dark brown sugar
½ cup (1 stick) SHEDD'S® Spread Country Crock
     Spread-Sticks
2 eggs
1 cup milk
1 cup raisins
1 carrot, shredded (about ¾ cup)

Preheat oven to 375°F. Grease 12-cup muffin pan or line with paper cupcake liners; set aside.

In large bowl, combine flour, baking powder, allspice and salt; set aside.

In another large bowl, with electric mixer, beat sugar and SHEDD'S® Spread Country Crock Spread on medium-high speed until light and fluffy, about 5 minutes. Beat in eggs, scraping side occasionally, until blended. Alternately beat in flour mixture and milk until blended. Stir in raisins and carrot. Evenly spoon batter into prepared pan.

Bake 18 minutes or until toothpick inserted in centers comes out clean. On wire rack, cool 10 minutes; remove from pan and cool completely.

Makes 12 muffins

CHOCOLATE STREUSEL PECAN MUFFINS

♥ ♥ ♥

TOPPING
¼ cup all-purpose flour
¼ cup packed brown sugar
¼ teaspoon ground cinnamon
2 tablespoons butter, melted
¼ cup chopped pecans

MUFFINS
1¾ cups (11.5-ounce package) NESTLÉ® TOLL HOUSE® Milk
    Chocolate Morsels, *divided*
⅓ cup milk
3 tablespoons butter
1 cup all-purpose flour
2 tablespoons granulated sugar
2 teaspoons baking powder
¼ teaspoon ground cinnamon
¾ cup chopped pecans
1 egg
½ teaspoon vanilla extract

FOR TOPPING
COMBINE flour, brown sugar, cinnamon and butter in small bowl with fork until mixture resembles coarse crumbs. Stir in nuts.

FOR MUFFINS
PREHEAT oven to 375°F. Grease or paper-line 12 muffin cups.

COMBINE *1 cup* morsels, milk and butter over hot (not boiling) water. Stir until morsels are melted and mixture is smooth.

COMBINE flour, granulated sugar, baking powder, cinnamon, pecans and *remaining* morsels in large bowl.

COMBINE egg, vanilla extract and melted morsel mixture in small bowl; stir into flour mixture just until moistened. Spoon into prepared muffin cups, filling ⅔ full. Sprinkle with topping.

BAKE for 20 to 25 minutes. Cool in pan for 5 minutes; remove to wire rack to cool completely.

Makes 12 muffins

LEMON POPPY SEED MUFFINS

♥ ♥ ♥

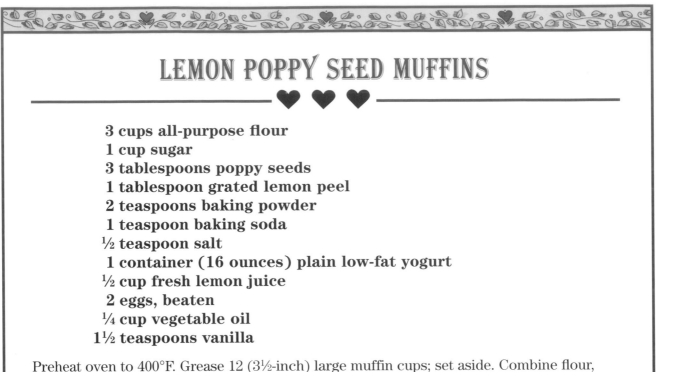

3 cups all-purpose flour
1 cup sugar
3 tablespoons poppy seeds
1 tablespoon grated lemon peel
2 teaspoons baking powder
1 teaspoon baking soda
½ teaspoon salt
1 container (16 ounces) plain low-fat yogurt
½ cup fresh lemon juice
2 eggs, beaten
¼ cup vegetable oil
1½ teaspoons vanilla

Preheat oven to 400°F. Grease 12 (3½-inch) large muffin cups; set aside. Combine flour, sugar, poppy seeds, lemon peel, baking powder, baking soda and salt in large bowl. Combine yogurt, lemon juice, eggs, oil and vanilla in small bowl until well blended. Stir into flour mixture just until moistened. Spoon into prepared muffin cups, filling ⅔ full. Bake 25 to 30 minutes or until toothpicks inserted into centers come out clean. Cool in pans on wire racks 5 minutes. Remove from pans. Cool on wire racks 10 minutes. Serve warm or cool completely.   *Makes 12 jumbo muffins*

Lemon Poppy Seed Muffins

BLUEBERRY MUFFINS

♥ ♥ ♥

1 cup fresh or thawed frozen blueberries
1¾ cups plus 1 tablespoon all-purpose flour, divided
2 teaspoons baking powder
1 teaspoon grated lemon peel
½ teaspoon salt
½ cup MOTT'S® Apple Sauce
½ cup sugar
1 whole egg
1 egg white
2 tablespoons vegetable oil
¼ cup skim milk

1. Preheat oven to 375°F. Line 12 (2½-inch) muffin cups with paper liners or spray with nonstick cooking spray.

2. In small bowl, toss blueberries with 1 tablespoon flour.

3. In large bowl, combine remaining 1¾ cups flour, baking powder, lemon peel and salt.

4. In another small bowl, combine apple sauce, sugar, whole egg, egg white and oil.

5. Stir apple sauce mixture into flour mixture alternately with milk. Mix just until moistened. Fold in blueberry mixture.

6. Spoon evenly into prepared muffin cups.

7. Bake 20 minutes or until toothpick inserted in centers comes out clean. Immediately remove from pan; cool on wire rack 10 minutes. Serve warm or cool completely.

Makes 12 servings

Blueberry Muffins

WHITE CHOCOLATE CHUNK MUFFINS

♥ ♥ ♥

2½ cups all-purpose flour
1 cup packed light brown sugar
⅓ cup unsweetened cocoa powder
2 teaspoons baking soda
½ teaspoon salt
1⅓ cups buttermilk
6 tablespoons butter, melted
2 eggs, beaten
1½ teaspoons vanilla
1½ cups chopped white chocolate

Preheat oven to 400°F. Grease 12 (3½-inch) large muffin cups; set aside.

Combine flour, sugar, cocoa, baking soda and salt in large bowl. Combine buttermilk, butter, eggs and vanilla in small bowl until blended. Stir into flour mixture just until moistened. Fold in white chocolate. Spoon into prepared muffin cups, filling half full.

Bake 25 to 30 minutes or until toothpicks inserted into centers come out clean. Cool in pan on wire rack 5 minutes. Remove from pan. Cool on wire rack 10 minutes. Serve warm or cool completely.
Makes 12 large muffins

White Chocolate Chunk Muffins

NUTMEG STRAWBERRY MUFFINS

♥ ♥ ♥

2 cups stemmed and halved (quartered if large) California
    strawberries (about 1 pint basket)
2 cups sugar, divided
3 cups flour
½ cup cornmeal
1 tablespoon nutmeg
1 teaspoon salt
1 teaspoon baking soda
1¼ cups vegetable oil
4 eggs, beaten
1 cup chopped walnuts

Preheat oven to 375°F. In bowl toss strawberries with 1 tablespoon of sugar; set aside. In large bowl mix remaining sugar, flour, cornmeal, nutmeg, salt and baking soda. Mix oil and eggs with strawberries; add to flour mixture with walnuts. Mix just to moisten dry ingredients. Measure ⅓ cup each into 24 paper-lined or greased 2¾-inch muffin tin cups. In small bowl mix 1 tablespoon each additional sugar and cornmeal with ¼ teaspoon additional nutmeg; sprinkle on muffin tops. Bake in center of oven about 25 minutes until springy to the touch and pick inserted into centers comes out clean. Serve warm or at room temperature. Cooled muffins can be wrapped and frozen up to 2 months.

Makes 24 muffins

Nutmeg Strawberry Bread: Divide batter between two greased 8½×4-inch loaf pans. Sprinkle tops with sugar mixture. Bake in preheated 375°F oven about 1 hour and 10 minutes or until pick inserted into center comes out clean. Cool on rack. Slice to serve. Makes 2 loaves.

Favorite recipe from **California Strawberry Commission**

Nutmeg Strawberry Muffins

GINGERBREAD STREUSEL RAISIN MUFFINS
♥ ♥ ♥

   1 cup raisins
½ cup boiling water
⅓ cup margarine or butter, softened
¾ cup GRANDMA'S® Molasses (Unsulphured)
   1 egg
   2 cups all-purpose flour
1½ teaspoons baking soda
   1 teaspoon cinnamon
   1 teaspoon ginger
½ teaspoon salt

TOPPING
⅓ cup all-purpose flour
¼ cup firmly packed brown sugar
¼ cup chopped nuts
   3 tablespoons margarine or butter
   1 teaspoon cinnamon

Preheat oven to 375°F. Grease bottoms only of 12 muffin cups or line with paper baking cups. In small bowl, cover raisins with boiling water; let stand 5 minutes. In large bowl, beat ⅓ cup margarine and molasses until fluffy. Add egg; beat well. Stir in 2 cups flour, baking soda, 1 teaspoon cinnamon, ginger and salt. Blend just until dry ingredients are moistened. Gently stir in raisins and water. Fill prepared muffin cups ¾ full. For topping, combine all ingredients in small bowl. Sprinkle over muffins.

Bake 20 to 25 minutes or until toothpick inserted in centers comes out clean. Cool 5 minutes; remove from pan. Serve warm. *Makes 12 muffins*

Gingerbread Streusel Raisin Muffins

BANANA WALNUT MUFFINS
♥ ♥ ♥

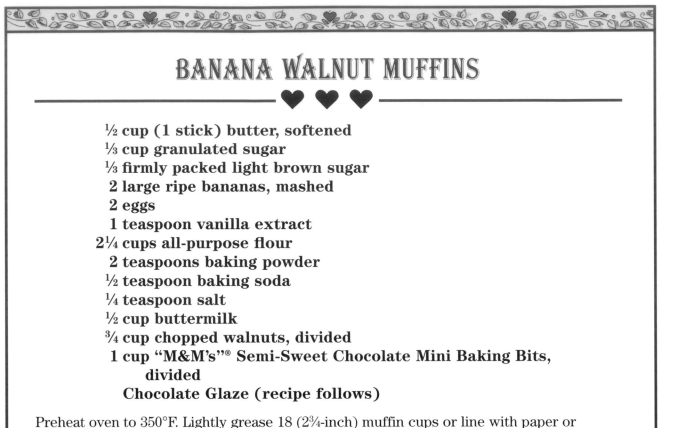

½ cup (1 stick) butter, softened
⅓ cup granulated sugar
⅓ firmly packed light brown sugar
2 large ripe bananas, mashed
2 eggs
1 teaspoon vanilla extract
2¼ cups all-purpose flour
2 teaspoons baking powder
½ teaspoon baking soda
¼ teaspoon salt
½ cup buttermilk
¾ cup chopped walnuts, divided
1 cup "M&M's"® Semi-Sweet Chocolate Mini Baking Bits, divided
Chocolate Glaze (recipe follows)

Preheat oven to 350°F. Lightly grease 18 (2¾-inch) muffin cups or line with paper or foil liners; set aside. In large bowl cream butter and sugars until light and fluffy; beat in bananas, eggs and vanilla. In medium bowl combine flour, baking powder, baking soda and salt. Alternately add one-third flour mixture and half of buttermilk to creamed mixture, ending with flour mixture. Stir in ½ cup walnuts. Divide batter evenly among prepared muffin cups. Sprinkle with ¾ cup "M&M's"® Semi-Sweet Chocolate Mini Baking Bits. Bake 20 to 25 minutes or until toothpick inserted in centers comes out clean. Cool completely on wire racks. Prepare Chocolate Glaze. Drizzle over muffins; sprinkle with remaining ¼ cup walnuts and remaining ¼ cup "M&M's"® Semi-Sweet Chocolate Mini Baking Bits. Store in tightly covered container.   *Makes 18 muffins*

CHOCOLATE GLAZE

1 cup powdered sugar
1 tablespoon plus 1 teaspoon unsweetened cocoa powder
1 tablespoon plus 1 teaspoon water
¾ teaspoon vanilla extract

In medium bowl combine powdered sugar and cocoa powder. Stir in water and vanilla; mix well.

MOCHA-MACADAMIA NUT MUFFINS

♥ ♥ ♥

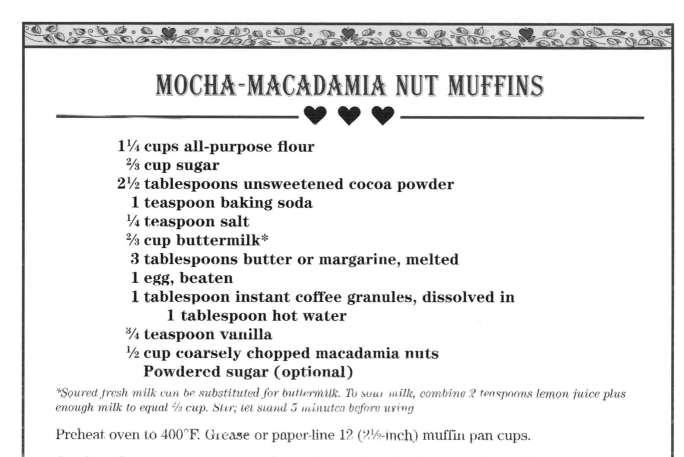

1¼ cups all-purpose flour

⅔ cup sugar

2½ tablespoons unsweetened cocoa powder

1 teaspoon baking soda

¼ teaspoon salt

⅔ cup buttermilk*

3 tablespoons butter or margarine, melted

1 egg, beaten

1 tablespoon instant coffee granules, dissolved in
    1 tablespoon hot water

¾ teaspoon vanilla

½ cup coarsely chopped macadamia nuts

Powdered sugar (optional)

*Soured fresh milk can be substituted for buttermilk. To sour milk, combine 2 teaspoons lemon juice plus enough milk to equal ⅔ cup. Stir; let stand 5 minutes before using.

Preheat oven to 400°F. Grease or paper-line 12 (2½-inch) muffin pan cups.

Combine flour, sugar, cocoa powder, baking soda and salt in large bowl. Whisk together buttermilk, butter, egg, coffee mixture and vanilla in small bowl until blended. Stir into flour mixture just until moistened. Fold in macadamia nuts. Spoon evenly into prepared muffin cups.

Bake 13 to 17 minutes or until toothpicks inserted into centers come out clean. Cool in muffin pan on wire rack 5 minutes. Remove from pan and cool on wire rack 10 minutes. Sprinkle with powdered sugar, if desired. *Makes 12 muffins*

Tasty Breakfast Treats

CINNAMON-DATE SCONES

♥ ♥ ♥

4 tablespoons sugar, divided
¼ teaspoon ground cinnamon
2 cups all-purpose flour
2½ teaspoons baking powder
½ teaspoon salt
5 tablespoons cold butter
½ cup chopped pitted dates
2 eggs
⅓ cup half-and-half or milk

Preheat oven to 425°F. Combine 2 tablespoons sugar and cinnamon in small bowl; set aside. Combine flour, remaining 2 tablespoons sugar, baking powder and salt in medium bowl. Cut in butter with pastry blender or 2 knives until mixture resembles coarse crumbs. Stir in dates.

Beat eggs in another small bowl with fork. Add half-and-half; beat until well combined. Reserve 1 tablespoon mixture in small cup. Stir remaining egg mixture into flour mixture. Stir until mixture forms soft dough that clings together and forms a ball.

Turn out dough onto well-floured surface. Knead dough gently 10 to 12 times. Roll out dough into 9×6-inch rectangle. Cut rectangle into 6 (3-inch) squares. Cut each square diagonally in half. Place triangles 2 inches apart on ungreased baking sheets. Brush with reserved egg mixture; sprinkle with reserved sugar mixture. Bake 10 to 12 minutes or until golden brown. Immediately remove from baking sheets; cool on wire racks 10 minutes. Serve warm.

Makes 12 scones

Cinnamon-Date Scones

BERRY-CHEESE BRAID

♥ ♥ ♥

DOUGH
       1 cup milk
       1 egg, lightly beaten
       3 tablespoons butter, softened
       1 teaspoon salt
       3 cups bread flour
       5 tablespoons sugar
    1½ teaspoons active dry yeast

FILLING
       1 package (8 ounces) cream cheese, at room temperature
       1 egg
      ¼ cup sugar
      ½ teaspoon vanilla
       1 cup fresh raspberries
       1 cup fresh blueberries

TOPPING
       1 tablespoon sugar

1. Measuring carefully, place all dough ingredients in bread machine pan in order specified by owner's manual. Program dough cycle setting; press start. (Do not use delay cycle.) Lightly grease 2 baking sheets; set aside.

2. For filling, beat cream cheese, egg, sugar and vanilla until well blended; set aside.

3. When cycle is complete, remove dough to lightly floured surface. If necessary, knead in additional bread flour to make dough easy to handle. Divide dough in half. Roll each half into 12×9-inch rectangle; carefully place rectangles on prepared baking sheets.

4. Spread filling lengthwise down center ⅓ of each dough rectangle, leaving 1-inch border at short ends. Sprinkle evenly with raspberries and blueberries. Fold 1-inch dough borders in toward centers. Make 5 cuts on each side of dough rectangles, just up to filling, to form 6 strips on each side. Gently fold strips in toward centers, alternating left and right, and allowing some filling to show through. Sprinkle braids with 1 tablespoon sugar. Cover with clean towels; let rise in warm, draft-free place 45 minutes or until doubled in size.

5. Preheat oven to 325°F. Bake braids 25 to 30 minutes or until golden brown. Remove from baking sheets; cool on wire racks. Serve at room temperature.

Makes 2 braids or 24 servings

Berry-Cheese Braid

CHOCOLATE CHIP COFFEECAKE

♥ ♥ ♥

3 cups all-purpose flour
⅓ cup sugar
2 envelopes FLEISCHMANN'S® RapidRise™ Yeast
1 teaspoon salt
½ cup milk
½ cup water
½ cup butter or margarine
2 eggs
¾ cup semi-sweet chocolate morsels
Chocolate Nut Topping (recipe follows)

In large bowl, combine 1 cup flour, sugar, undissolved yeast and salt. Heat milk, water and butter until very warm (120° to 130°F). Gradually add to dry ingredients. Beat 2 minutes at medium speed of electric mixer, scraping bowl occasionally. Add eggs and 1 cup flour; beat 2 minutes at high speed, scraping bowl occasionally. Stir in chocolate morsels and remaining flour to make a soft batter. Turn into greased 13×9×2-inch baking pan. Cover; let rise in warm, draft-free place until doubled in size, about 1 hour.

Bake at 400°F for 15 minutes; remove from oven and sprinkle with Chocolate Nut Topping. Return to oven and bake additional 10 minutes or until done. Cool in pan for 10 minutes. Remove from pan; cool on wire rack. *Makes 1 cake*

Chocolate Nut Topping: In medium bowl, cut ½ cup butter into ⅔ cup all-purpose flour until crumbly. Stir in ⅔ cup sugar, 2 teaspoons ground cinnamon, 1 cup semi-sweet chocolate morsels and 1 cup chopped pecans.

Chocolate Chip Coffeecake

GOOEY CARAMEL AND CHOCOLATE PECAN ROLLS

❤ ❤ ❤

2 loaves (1 pound each) frozen white bread dough
1 jar (12 ounces) caramel ice cream topping
⅔ cup coarsely chopped pecans
1 cup semisweet chocolate chips, divided
4 tablespoons butter, divided

1. Thaw bread dough according to package directions.

2. Preheat oven to 375°F. Divide caramel topping evenly between two 9-inch round cake pans; spread in thin layer. Sprinkle pecans evenly over caramel.

3. Microwave ⅔ cup chocolate chips and 2 tablespoons butter in medium microwavable bowl at HIGH (100% power) 30 seconds; stir. Microwave at additional 20-second intervals, if necessary, stirring until smooth; set aside.

4. On lightly floured surface, roll one loaf bread dough into 12×8-inch rectangle. Spread half chocolate mixture over dough. Beginning from the long side, roll up jelly-roll style to form 12-inch log, pinching seam to seal. Slice into 12 rolls; arrange cut side down in 1 prepared pan. Repeat with remaining dough and chocolate mixture.

5. Cover; let rise in warm place until nearly doubled, about 1 hour. Uncover; bake 20 to 25 minutes. Immediately invert onto serving plates.

6. Melt remaining ⅓ cup chocolate chips and 2 tablespoons butter in microwave as directed in step 3. Drizzle over warm rolls. *Makes 24 rolls*

Gooey Caramel and
Chocolate Pecan Rolls

GREEN ONION CREAM CHEESE BREAKFAST BISCUITS

♥ ♥ ♥

2 cups all-purpose flour
1 tablespoon baking powder
1 tablespoon sugar
¾ teaspoon salt
1 package (3 ounces) cream cheese
¼ cup shortening
½ cup finely chopped green onions
⅔ cup milk

1. Preheat oven to 450°F.

2. Combine flour, baking powder, sugar and salt in medium bowl. Cut in cream cheese and shortening with pastry blender or two knives until mixture resembles coarse crumbs. Stir in green onions.

3. Make well in center of flour mixture. Add milk; stir until mixture forms soft dough that clings together and forms a ball.

4. Turn out dough onto well-floured surface. Knead dough gently 10 to 12 times.

5. Roll or pat dough to ½-inch thickness. Cut dough with floured 3-inch biscuit cutter.

6. Place biscuits 2 inches apart on ungreased large baking sheet. Bake 10 to 12 minutes or until tops and bottoms are golden brown. Serve warm.   *Makes 8 biscuits*

*Green Onion Cream Cheese
Breakfast Biscuits*

MINI CHIP HARVEST RING

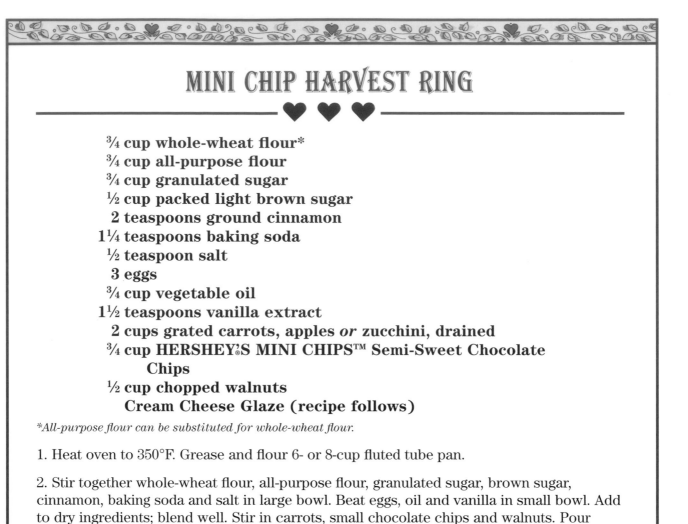

♥ ♥ ♥

¾ cup whole-wheat flour*
¾ cup all-purpose flour
¾ cup granulated sugar
½ cup packed light brown sugar
2 teaspoons ground cinnamon
1¼ teaspoons baking soda
½ teaspoon salt
3 eggs
¾ cup vegetable oil
1½ teaspoons vanilla extract
2 cups grated carrots, apples *or* zucchini, drained
¾ cup HERSHEY'S MINI CHIPS™ Semi-Sweet Chocolate
    Chips
½ cup chopped walnuts
Cream Cheese Glaze (recipe follows)

All-purpose flour can be substituted for whole-wheat flour.

1. Heat oven to 350°F. Grease and flour 6- or 8-cup fluted tube pan.

2. Stir together whole-wheat flour, all-purpose flour, granulated sugar, brown sugar, cinnamon, baking soda and salt in large bowl. Beat eggs, oil and vanilla in small bowl. Add to dry ingredients; blend well. Stir in carrots, small chocolate chips and walnuts. Pour batter into prepared pan.

3. Bake 45 to 50 minutes or until wooden pick inserted in center comes out clean. Cool 30 minutes; remove from pan to wire rack.

4. Prepare Cream Cheese Glaze; spread over top of cake, allowing glaze to run down sides. Garnish as desired. *Makes 8 to 10 servings*

CREAM CHEESE GLAZE

1½ ounces (½ of 3-ounce package) cream cheese, softened
¾ cup powdered sugar
2 teaspoons milk
½ teaspoon vanilla extract

1. Beat cream cheese, powdered sugar, milk and vanilla in small bowl until smooth and of desired consistency. Add additional milk, ½ teaspoon at a time, if needed.

BUTTERMILK DOUGHNUTS

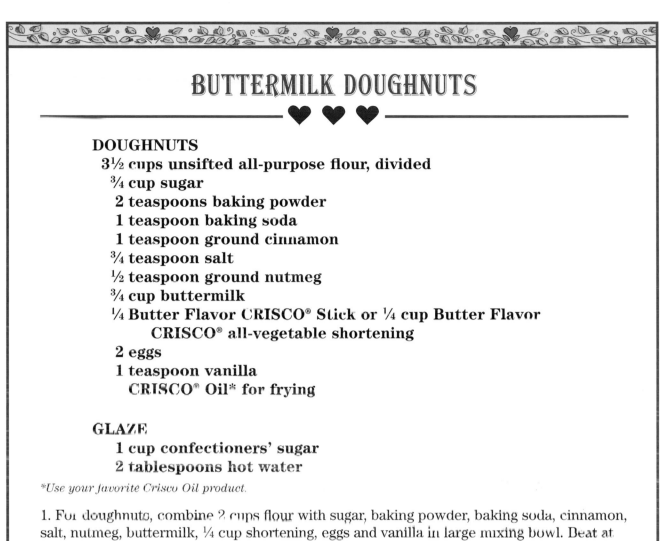

♥ ♥ ♥

DOUGHNUTS
3½ cups unsifted all-purpose flour, divided
¾ cup sugar
2 teaspoons baking powder
1 teaspoon baking soda
1 teaspoon ground cinnamon
¾ teaspoon salt
½ teaspoon ground nutmeg
¾ cup buttermilk
¼ Butter Flavor CRISCO® Stick or ¼ cup Butter Flavor
   CRISCO® all-vegetable shortening
2 eggs
1 teaspoon vanilla
   CRISCO® Oil* for frying

GLAZE
1 cup confectioners' sugar
2 tablespoons hot water

*Use your favorite Crisco Oil product.

1. For doughnuts, combine 2 cups flour with sugar, baking powder, baking soda, cinnamon, salt, nutmeg, buttermilk, ¼ cup shortening, eggs and vanilla in large mixing bowl. Beat at low speed of electric mixer until blended. Beat at medium speed 2 minutes. Stir in remaining flour. Chill several hours or overnight.

2. Divide dough in half. Sprinkle lightly with flour. Roll each half to slightly less than ½-inch thickness on well-floured board. Cut with floured 2¾- to 3-inch doughnut cutter. Reserve doughnut holes.

3. Heat 2 inches oil to 375°F in deep-fat fryer or deep saucepan. Fry a few doughnuts at a time in hot shortening, 1 minute on each side, or until golden brown. Fry doughnut holes 1 to 1½ minutes total time. Drain on paper towels. Serve plain, dip tops in glaze or cool and shake in plastic bag of confectioners' sugar.

4. For glaze, combine confectioners' sugar and water in small bowl; stir until smooth. Dip tops of doughnuts in glaze. Invert on wire racks until glaze is set.

Makes 1½ to 2 dozen doughnuts and doughnut holes

HONEY CURRANT SCONES

♥ ♥ ♥

2½ cups all-purpose flour
2 teaspoons grated orange peel
1 teaspoon baking powder
½ teaspoon baking soda
½ teaspoon salt
½ cup cold butter or margarine
½ cup currants
½ cup sour cream
⅓ cup honey
1 egg, slightly beaten

Preheat oven to 375°F. Grease baking sheet; set aside.

Combine flour, orange peel, baking powder, baking soda and salt in large bowl. Cut in butter with pastry blender or 2 knives until mixture resembles coarse crumbs. Add currants. Combine sour cream, honey and egg in medium bowl until well blended. Stir into flour mixture until soft dough forms. Turn out dough onto lightly floured surface. Knead dough 10 times. Shape dough into 8-inch square. Cut into 4 squares; cut each square diagonally in half, making 8 triangles. Place triangles 1 inch apart on prepared baking sheet.

Bake 15 to 20 minutes or until golden brown and wooden pick inserted in centers comes out clean. Remove from baking sheet. Cool on wire rack 10 minutes. Serve warm or cool completely.

Makes 8 scones

Favorite recipe from **National Honey Board**

Honey Currant Scones

THREE-BERRY KUCHEN

♥ ♥ ♥

1¾ cups all-purpose flour, divided
2 teaspoons baking powder
½ teaspoon baking soda
½ teaspoon salt
⅔ cup MOTT'S® Apple Sauce
4 egg whites
¼ cup plain nonfat yogurt
2 tablespoons granulated sugar
1 teaspoon grated lemon peel
2 cups assorted fresh or thawed frozen blueberries,
    raspberries and blackberries
¼ cup firmly packed light brown sugar
2 tablespoons margarine

1. Preheat oven to 350°F. Spray 10-inch round cake pan with nonstick cooking spray.

2. In small bowl, combine 1½ cups flour, baking powder, baking soda and salt.

3. In large bowl, whisk together apple sauce, egg whites, yogurt, granulated sugar and lemon peel.

4. Add flour mixture to apple sauce mixture; stir until well blended. Spread batter into prepared pan.

5. Sprinkle berries over batter. Combine remaining ¼ cup flour and brown sugar in small bowl. Cut in margarine with pastry blender or fork until mixture resembles coarse crumbs. Sprinkle over berries.

6. Bake 50 to 55 minutes or until lightly browned. Cool on wire rack 20 minutes. Serve warm or cool completely. Cut into 9 slices.   *Makes 9 servings*

Three-Berry Kuchen

PEANUT BUTTER & CHOCOLATE PULL-APART ROLLS

❤ ❤ ❤

DOUGH
- ½ cup milk
- ⅓ cup water (70 to 80°F)
- ¼ cup creamy peanut butter, at room temperature
- ½ teaspoon salt
- 2¼ cups bread flour
- ¼ cup sugar
- 1½ teaspoons FLEISCHMANN'S® Bread Machine Yeast

FILLING
- ½ cup (3 ounces) semisweet chocolate pieces
- 2 tablespoons creamy peanut butter

ICING
- ½ cup sifted powdered sugar
- 1 tablespoon creamy peanut butter or cocoa powder
- 2 to 4 teaspoons milk

To make dough, add dough ingredients to bread machine pan in the order suggested by manufacturer. Select dough/manual cycle.

To make filling, combine filling ingredients in small bowl; blend well. To shape and fill, when cycle is complete, remove dough to floured surface. If necessary, knead in additional flour to make dough easy to handle.

Roll dough into 14-inch circle. Cut into 6 wedges; place filling, dividing evenly, at wide end of each wedge. Beginning at wide end, roll up tightly; curve to form crescent. Arrange crescents, seam side down, in spoke fashion on greased large baking sheet. Pinch ends at center to seal. Cover and let rise in warm, draft-free place until doubled in size, about 30 to 45 minutes. Bake at 375°F for 15 to 20 minutes or until done. Remove from pan; cool on wire rack.

To make icing, combine icing ingredients in small bowl; stir until smooth. Drizzle on rolls.

Makes 6 rolls

Note: Dough can be prepared in all size bread machines.

Peanut Butter & Chocolate
Pull-Apart Rolls

ENGLISH-STYLE SCONES

❤ ❤ ❤

3 eggs
½ cup heavy cream
1½ teaspoons vanilla
2 cups all-purpose flour
2 teaspoons baking powder
¼ teaspoon salt
¼ cup cold butter
¼ cup finely chopped pitted dates
¼ cup golden raisins or currants
1 teaspoon water
6 tablespoons no-sugar-added orange marmalade fruit
     spread
6 tablespoons softly whipped cream or crème fraîche

Preheat oven to 375°F. Beat 2 eggs with cream and vanilla; set aside. Combine flour, baking powder and salt in medium bowl. Cut in butter with pastry blender or two knives until mixture resembles coarse crumbs. Stir in dates and raisins. Add egg mixture; mix just until dry ingredients are moistened. With floured hands, knead dough four times on lightly floured surface. Place dough on greased cookie sheet; pat into 8-inch circle. With sharp wet knife, gently score dough into six wedges, cutting ¾ of the way into dough. Beat remaining egg with water; brush lightly over dough. Bake 18 to 20 minutes or until golden brown. Cool 5 minutes on wire rack. Cut into wedges. Serve warm with marmalade and whipped cream. *Makes 6 scones*

English-Style Scone

DONNA'S HEAVENLY ORANGE CHIP SCONES

♥ ♥ ♥

4 cups all-purpose flour
1 cup granulated sugar
4 teaspoons baking powder
½ teaspoon baking soda
½ teaspoon salt
1 cup (6 ounces) NESTLÉ® TOLL HOUSE® Semi-Sweet
    Chocolate Mini Morsels
1 cup golden raisins
1 tablespoon grated orange peel
1 cup (2 sticks) unsalted butter, cut into pieces and
    softened
1 cup buttermilk
3 eggs, *divided*
1 teaspoon orange extract
1 tablespoon milk
   Icing (recipe follows)

PREHEAT oven to 350°F. Lightly grease baking sheets.

COMBINE flour, granulated sugar, baking powder, baking soda and salt in large bowl. Add morsels, raisins and orange peel; mix well. Cut in butter with pastry blender or two knives until mixture resembles coarse crumbs. Combine buttermilk, *2 eggs* and orange extract in small bowl. Pour buttermilk mixture into flour mixture; mix just until a sticky dough is formed. Do not overmix. Drop by ¼ cupfuls onto prepared baking sheets. Combine *remaining* egg and milk in small bowl. Brush egg mixture over top of dough.

BAKE for 18 to 22 minutes or until wooden pick inserted in center comes out clean. For best results, bake one baking sheet at a time. Cool on wire racks for 10 minutes. Drizzle scones with icing. Serve warm.
       Makes 2 dozen scones

Icing: COMBINE 2 cups powdered sugar, ¼ cup orange juice, 1 tablespoon grated orange peel and 1 teaspoon orange extract in medium bowl. Mix until smooth.

Donna's Heavenly Orange Chip Scones

TRIPLE CHOCOLATE STICKY BUNS

♥ ♥ ♥

DOUGH
¼ cup water
½ cup sour cream
1 egg
3 tablespoons butter, softened
1 teaspoon salt
2¾ cups bread flour
⅓ cup unsweetened cocoa powder
¼ cup sugar
2 teaspoons active dry yeast

TOPPING
⅓ cup packed brown sugar
¼ cup butter
2 tablespoons light corn syrup
1 tablespoon unsweetened cocoa powder

FILLING
⅓ cup packed brown sugar
3 tablespoons butter, softened
½ teaspoon ground cinnamon
½ to ¾ cup coarsely chopped walnuts, toasted*
½ cup semisweet chocolate chips

To toast walnuts, spread in single layer on baking sheet. Bake in preheated 350°F oven 8 to 10 minutes or until golden brown, stirring frequently.

1. Measuring carefully, place all dough ingredients in bread machine pan in order specified by owner's manual. Program dough cycle; press start. *Do not use delay cycle.* Lightly grease 9-inch round cake pan; set aside.

2. While dough is rising, prepare topping by combining brown sugar, butter, corn syrup and cocoa powder in small saucepan. Cook over medium heat, stirring constantly, until sugar is dissolved and mixture bubbles around edge. Pour into prepared pan; set aside.

3. For filling, combine brown sugar, butter and cinnamon in small bowl; set aside.

continued on page 190

Triple Chocolate Sticky Bun

4. When cycle is complete, punch down dough and remove to lightly floured surface. If necessary, knead in additional bread flour to make dough easy to handle. Roll into 12×8-inch rectangle. Spread with filling mixture. Sprinkle with walnuts and chocolate chips. Starting at long side, roll up tightly, jelly-roll fashion. Pinch seam to seal. Cut crosswise into 12 slices. Arrange over topping in pan. Cover with greased waxed paper. Let rise in warm, draft-free place 45 to 60 minutes or until doubled in size.

5. Place piece of foil on oven rack to catch drippings. Preheat oven to 375°F. Bake about 25 minutes or just until buns in center of pan are firm to the touch. *Do not overbake.* Immediately invert onto serving plate. Serve warm or at room temperature.

Makes 12 rolls

GRANDMA'S APPLE FRITTERS
♥ ♥ ♥

CRISCO® Oil for deep frying
1 egg, lightly beaten
½ cup milk
1 tablespoon CRISCO® Oil*
1 cup diced peeled apples or drained crushed pineapple
1 cup all-purpose flour
1 tablespoon granulated sugar
1 teaspoon baking powder
¼ teaspoon salt
1 cup confectioners' sugar
1 teaspoon ground cinnamon

Use your favorite Crisco Oil product.

1. Heat 2 to 3 inches oil to 365°F in deep fryer or deep saucepan.

2. Combine egg and milk in large bowl. Stir in 1 tablespoon oil and apples or pineapple.

3. Combine flour, granulated sugar, baking powder and salt. Add to egg mixture. Stir just until mixed.

4. Drop by tablespoonfuls, a few at a time, into oil heated to 365°F. Fry about 4 minutes or until golden brown. Turn as needed for even browning. Remove with slotted metal spoon. Drain on paper towels.

5. Combine confectioners' sugar and cinnamon in small bowl. Roll fritters in mixture. Serve warm.

Makes 6 to 8 servings

CREAMY CINNAMON ROLLS

♥ ♥ ♥

2 (1-pound) loaves frozen bread dough, thawed
⅔ cup (one-half 14-ounce can) EAGLE BRAND® Sweetened
Condensed Milk* (NOT evaporated milk), divided
1 cup chopped pecans
2 teaspoons ground cinnamon
1 cup sifted powdered sugar
½ teaspoon vanilla extract
Additional chopped pecans, if desired

*Use remaining Eagle Brand as a dip for fruit. Pour into storage container and store tightly covered in refrigerator for up to 1 week.

1. On lightly floured surface, roll each bread dough loaf into 12×9-inch rectangle. Spread ⅓ cup Eagle Brand over dough rectangles. Sprinkle rectangles with 1 cup pecans and cinnamon. Roll up jelly-roll style starting from short side. Cut each log into 6 slices.

2. Generously grease 13×9-inch baking pan. Place rolls cut sides down in pan. Cover loosely with greased waxed paper and then with plastic wrap. Chill overnight. Cover and chill remaining Eagle Brand.

3. To bake, let pan of rolls stand at room temperature 30 minutes. Preheat oven to 350°F. Bake 30 to 35 minutes or until golden brown. Cool in pan 5 minutes; loosen edges and remove rolls from pan.

4. Meanwhile for frosting, in small mixing bowl, combine powdered sugar, remaining ⅓ cup Eagle Brand and vanilla. Drizzle frosting over warm rolls. Sprinkle with additional chopped pecans, if desired.

Makes 12 rolls

Prep Time: 20 minutes
Bake Time: 30 to 35 minutes
Chill Time: Overnight
Cool Time: 5 minutes

Savory Temptations

TEX-MEX QUICK BREAD

♥ ♥ ♥

1½ cups all-purpose flour
1 cup (4 ounces) shredded Monterey Jack cheese
½ cup cornmeal
½ cup sun-dried tomatoes, coarsely chopped
1 can (about 4 ounces) black olives, drained and chopped
¼ cup sugar
1½ teaspoons baking powder
1 teaspoon baking soda
1 cup milk
1 can (about 4 ounces) green chilies, drained and chopped
¼ cup olive oil
1 egg, beaten

1. Preheat oven to 325°F. Grease 9×5-inch loaf pan or four 5×3-inch loaf pans; set aside.

2. Combine flour, cheese, cornmeal, tomatoes, olives, sugar, baking powder and baking soda in large bowl.

3. Combine remaining ingredients in small bowl. Add to flour mixture; stir just until combined. Pour into prepared pan. Bake 9×5-inch loaf 45 minutes and 5×3-inch loaves 30 minutes or until toothpick inserted near center of loaf comes out clean. Cool in pan 15 minutes. Remove from pan and cool on wire rack.

Makes 1 large loaf or 4 small loaves

Muffin Variation: Preheat oven to 375°F. Spoon batter into 12 well-greased muffin cups. Bake 20 minutes or until toothpick inserted into centers of muffins comes out clean. Makes 12 muffins.

Tex-Mex Quick Bread

HONEY SWEET POTATO BISCUITS

♥ ♥ ♥

2 cups all-purpose flour
1 tablespoon baking powder
½ teaspoon salt
¼ cup vegetable shortening
1 tablespoon grated orange peel
1 tablespoon grated lemon peel
¾ cup mashed cooked sweet potato (1 large sweet potato
    baked until tender, peeled and mashed)
⅓ cup honey
½ cup milk (about)

Combine flour, baking powder and salt in large bowl. Cut in shortening until mixture is size of small peas. Add orange and lemon peels, sweet potato and honey; mix well. Add enough milk to make soft, but not sticky, dough. Knead 3 or 4 times on lightly floured surface. Pat dough to 1-inch thickness and cut into 2¼-inch rounds. Place on ungreased baking sheet.

Bake in preheated 400°F oven 15 to 18 minutes or until lightly browned. Serve warm.

Makes 10 biscuits

Favorite recipe from **National Honey Board**

SAVORY PULL APART BISCUITS

♥ ♥ ♥

2 tablespoons butter or margarine
1 tablespoon minced onion
2 tablespoons grated Parmesan cheese
½ teaspoon TABASCO® brand Pepper Sauce
1 (8-ounce) package refrigerated biscuits

Melt butter in small saucepan. Add onion and cook until tender. Stir in cheese and TABASCO® Sauce; remove from heat. Separate biscuits. Dip biscuit tops in butter mixture and arrange biscuits buttered side up in lightly greased 8-inch round cake pan, making sure sides of biscuits touch. Bake 10 to 15 minutes or until golden. Serve warm.

Makes 10 biscuits

Honey Sweet Potato Biscuits

FAST PESTO FOCACCIA

♥ ♥ ♥

1 can (10 ounces) pizza crust dough
2 tablespoons prepared pesto
4 sun-dried tomatoes packed in oil, drained

1. Preheat oven to 425°F. Lightly grease 8×8×2-inch pan. Unroll pizza dough; fold in half and pat into pan.

2. Spread pesto evenly over dough. Chop tomatoes or snip with kitchen scissors; sprinkle over pesto. Press tomatoes into dough. Make indentations in dough every 2 inches using wooden spoon handle.

3. Bake 10 to 12 minutes or until golden brown. Cut into squares and serve warm or at room temperature.

Makes 16 squares

Prep and Cook Time: 20 minutes

SOUTHWESTERN SAUSAGE DROP BISCUITS

♥ ♥ ♥

1 pound BOB EVANS® Zesty Hot Roll Sausage
3 cups all-purpose (biscuit) baking mix
1¼ cups (5 ounces) shredded sharp Cheddar cheese
1 cup seeded diced fresh or drained canned tomatoes
1 cup chopped green onions
1 cup milk
¼ teaspoon paprika
Dash cayenne pepper
Butter (optional)

Preheat oven to 350°F. Crumble and cook sausage in medium skillet until browned. Drain on paper towels. Combine sausage and remaining ingredients except butter in large bowl; mix well. Shape dough into 2-inch balls; place on ungreased baking sheet. Bake 12 minutes or until golden. Serve hot with butter, if desired. Refrigerate leftovers.

Makes about 2 dozen small biscuits

Fast Pesto Focaccia

HERB-CHEESE BISCUIT LOAF

♥ ♥ ♥

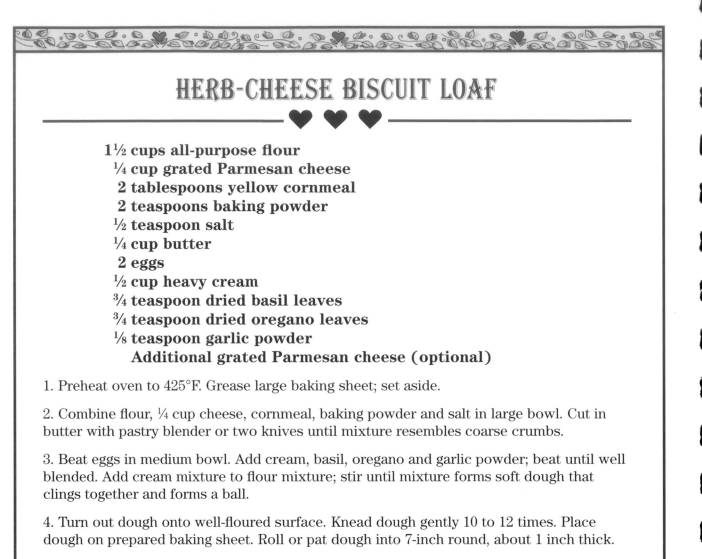

        1½ cups all-purpose flour
        ¼ cup grated Parmesan cheese
        2 tablespoons yellow cornmeal
        2 teaspoons baking powder
        ½ teaspoon salt
        ¼ cup butter
        2 eggs
        ½ cup heavy cream
        ¾ teaspoon dried basil leaves
        ¾ teaspoon dried oregano leaves
        ⅛ teaspoon garlic powder
        Additional grated Parmesan cheese (optional)

1. Preheat oven to 425°F. Grease large baking sheet; set aside.

2. Combine flour, ¼ cup cheese, cornmeal, baking powder and salt in large bowl. Cut in butter with pastry blender or two knives until mixture resembles coarse crumbs.

3. Beat eggs in medium bowl. Add cream, basil, oregano and garlic powder; beat until well blended. Add cream mixture to flour mixture; stir until mixture forms soft dough that clings together and forms a ball.

4. Turn out dough onto well-floured surface. Knead dough gently 10 to 12 times. Place dough on prepared baking sheet. Roll or pat dough into 7-inch round, about 1 inch thick.

5. Starting from center, score top of dough into 8 wedges with tip of sharp knife, taking care not to cut completely through dough. Sprinkle with additional cheese, if desired.

6. Bake 20 to 25 minutes or until wooden toothpick inserted in center comes out clean. Cool on baking sheet on wire rack 10 minutes. Serve warm.   *Makes 8 servings*

Herb-Cheese Biscuit Loaf

SUN-DRIED TOMATO SCONES

❤ ❤ ❤

2 cups buttermilk baking mix
¼ cup (1 ounce) grated Parmesan cheese
1½ teaspoons dried basil
⅔ cup reduced-fat (2%) milk
½ cup chopped drained oil-packed sun-dried tomatoes
¼ cup chopped green onions

1. Preheat oven to 450°F. Combine baking mix, cheese and basil in medium bowl.

2. Stir in milk, tomatoes and onions. Mix just until dry ingredients are moistened. Drop by heaping teaspoonfuls onto greased baking sheet.

3. Bake 8 to 10 minutes or until light golden brown. Remove baking sheet to cooling rack; let stand 5 minutes. Remove scones and serve warm or at room temperature.

Makes 1½ dozen scones

Prep and Cook Time: 20 minutes

SPICY ONION BREAD

❤ ❤ ❤

2 tablespoons instant minced onion
⅓ cup water
1½ cups biscuit mix
1 egg, lightly beaten
½ cup milk
½ teaspoon TABASCO® brand Pepper Sauce
2 tablespoons butter, melted
½ teaspoon caraway seeds (optional)

Preheat oven to 400°F. Soak instant minced onion in water 5 minutes. Combine biscuit mix, egg, milk and TABASCO® Sauce in large bowl and stir until blended. Stir in onion. Turn into greased 8-inch pie plate. Brush with melted butter. Sprinkle with caraway seeds. Bake 20 to 25 minutes or until golden brown.

Makes 8 servings

Sun-Dried Tomato Scones

TOMATO-ARTICHOKE FOCACCIA

♥ ♥ ♥

1 package (16 ounces) hot roll mix
2 tablespoons wheat bran
1¼ cups hot water
4 teaspoons olive oil, divided
1 cup thinly sliced onions
2 cloves garlic, minced
4 ounces dry sun-dried tomatoes, rehydrated* and cut into strips
1 cup canned artichoke hearts, sliced
1 tablespoon minced fresh rosemary
2 tablespoons freshly grated Parmesan cheese

*To rehydrate sun-dried tomatoes, simply pour 1 cup boiling water over tomatoes in small heatproof bowl. Let tomatoes soak 5 to 10 minutes until softened; drain well.

1. Preheat oven to 400°F.

2. Combine dry ingredients and yeast packet from hot roll mix in large bowl. Add bran; mix well. Stir in hot water and 2 teaspoons oil. Knead dough about 5 minutes or until ingredients are blended.

3. Spray 15½×11½-inch baking pan or 14-inch pizza pan with nonstick cooking spray. Press dough onto bottom of prepared pan. Cover; let rise 15 minutes.

4. Heat 1 teaspoon oil in medium skillet over low heat. Add onions and garlic; cook and stir 2 to 3 minutes until onions are tender. Brush surface of dough with remaining 1 teaspoon oil. Top dough with onion mixture, tomatoes, artichokes and rosemary. Sprinkle with Parmesan.

5. Bake 25 to 30 minutes or until lightly browned on top. To serve, cut into squares.

Makes 16 servings

STUFFIN' MUFFINS

♥ ♥ ♥

⅔ cup dark or golden raisins
1¾ cups nonfat milk
2 tablespoons olive oil or walnut oil
½ cup finely diced Golden Delicious apple
½ cup finely chopped California walnuts
⅓ cup unsweetened applesauce
2 teaspoons dried sage
1 tablespoon sugar
1½ teaspoons salt
⅛ teaspoon black pepper
2½ cups all-purpose flour
1 tablespoon baking powder

In small bowl, cover raisins with water and let sit 1 minute; drain. Let raisins stand for 30 minutes to absorb the moisture that remains on their skins.

Preheat oven to 400°F. Grease standard muffin tins or line with cupcake papers.

In medium bowl, whisk together milk, oil, apple, walnuts, applesauce, sage, sugar, salt and pepper. In small bowl, combine flour and baking powder, sift onto piece of waxed paper. Add flour mixture and raisins to milk mixture and stir with fork until batter is blended. Spoon into prepared muffin tins, filling each cup almost full. Bake 25 to 30 minutes, or until wooden pick inserted in center of muffin comes out clean. Remove from tins and transfer to wire racks to cool slightly; serve warm.   *Makes 12 to 14 muffins*

Favorite recipe from **Walnut Marketing Board**

CORN BREAD

♥ ♥ ♥

1 cup all-purpose flour
1 cup yellow cornmeal
⅓ cup sugar
2 teaspoons baking powder
½ teaspoon salt
1 cup milk
⅓ cup vegetable oil
1 egg

1. Preheat oven to 400°F. Grease 8-inch square baking pan.

2. Combine flour, cornmeal, sugar, baking powder and salt in large bowl; set aside. Combine milk, oil and egg in small bowl until blended. Stir milk mixture into flour mixture just until moistened. Spread batter evenly in prepared pan.

3. Bake 20 to 25 minutes or until golden brown and toothpick inserted in center comes out clean. Cut into squares. Serve warm. *Makes 9 servings*

Corn Muffins: Preheat oven to 400°F. Prepare batter as directed in step 2, except spoon batter into 12 (2½-inch) greased or paper-lined muffin pan cups. Bake 20 minutes or until golden brown and toothpicks inserted into centers come out clean. Immediately remove from pan; cool on wire rack 10 minutes. Serve warm. Makes 12 muffins.

Corn Sticks: Preheat oven to 425°F. Heat cast-iron corn stick pan in oven while preparing batter as directed in step 2. Carefully brush hot pan with additional vegetable oil before spooning half of batter into prepared pan. Bake 10 to 15 minutes or until lightly browned. Immediately remove from pan; cool on wire racks 10 minutes. Repeat with remaining half of batter. Serve warm. Makes 14 corn sticks.

Corn Bread, Corn Muffins
and Corn Sticks

PICNIC PIZZA BISCUITS

♥ ♥ ♥

1 can (10 ounces) refrigerated buttermilk biscuits
1 pound hot Italian sausage, casings removed
½ cup chopped onion
½ cup sliced mushrooms
½ cup chopped green bell pepper
½ cup (2 ounces) shredded mozzarella cheese
¼ cup marinara or pizza sauce
2 tablespoons *French's*® Napa Valley Style Dijon Mustard

1. Preheat oven to 375°F. Separate biscuits; pat or roll into 10 (4-inch) circles on floured surface. Press circles into 12-cup muffin pan.

2. Cook sausage in large nonstick skillet over high heat 5 minutes or until browned, stirring to separate meat; drain fat. Add onion, mushrooms and bell pepper; cook and stir 3 minutes or until vegetables are tender. Stir in cheese, sauce and mustard; mix well.

3. Mound filling evenly in biscuits. Bake 20 minutes or until biscuits are browned. Serve warm or at room temperature. *Makes 10 servings*

Prep Time: 30 minutes
Cook Time: 25 minutes

BOSTON BROWN BREAD

♥ ♥ ♥

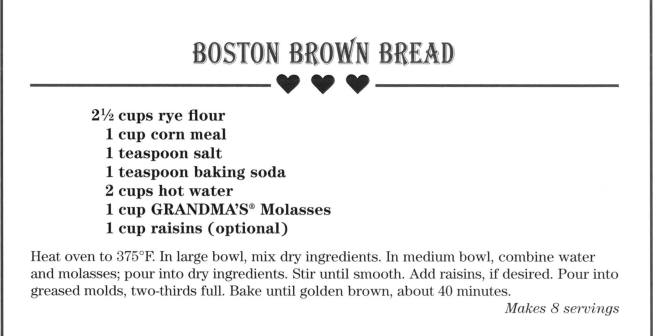

2½ cups rye flour
1 cup corn meal
1 teaspoon salt
1 teaspoon baking soda
2 cups hot water
1 cup GRANDMA'S® Molasses
1 cup raisins (optional)

Heat oven to 375°F. In large bowl, mix dry ingredients. In medium bowl, combine water and molasses; pour into dry ingredients. Stir until smooth. Add raisins, if desired. Pour into greased molds, two-thirds full. Bake until golden brown, about 40 minutes.

Makes 8 servings

Picnic Pizza Biscuits

BROCCOLI & CHEDDAR MUFFINS

❤ ❤ ❤

3 cups buttermilk baking and pancake mix
2 eggs, lightly beaten
⅔ cup milk
1 teaspoon dried basil
1 cup (4 ounces) shredded Cheddar cheese
1 box (10 ounces) BIRDS EYE® frozen Chopped Broccoli,
   thawed and drained

• Preheat oven to 350°F. Combine baking mix, eggs, milk and basil. Mix until moistened. (Do not overmix.)

• Add cheese and broccoli; stir just to combine. Add salt and pepper to taste.

• Spray 12 muffin cups with nonstick cooking spray. Pour batter into muffin cups. Bake 25 to 30 minutes or until golden brown.

• Cool 5 minutes in pan. Loosen sides of muffins with knife; remove from pan and serve warm.   *Makes 1 dozen large muffins*

Prep Time: 5 to 10 minutes
Bake Time: 25 to 30 minutes

Southwestern Corn Muffins: Prepare 1 box corn muffin mix according to package directions; add ⅔ cup BIRDS EYE® frozen Corn and 1 teaspoon chili powder to batter. Mix well; bake according to package directions.

Broccoli & Cheddar Muffins

CHIVE WHOLE WHEAT DROP BISCUITS

♥ ♥ ♥

1¼ cups whole wheat flour
¾ cup all-purpose flour
3 tablespoons toasted wheat germ, divided
1 tablespoon baking powder
1 tablespoon chopped fresh chives *or* 1 teaspoon dried chives
2 teaspoons sugar
3 tablespoons cold margarine
1 cup fat-free (skim) milk
½ cup shredded low-fat process American cheese

1. Preheat oven to 450°F. Spray baking sheet with nonstick cooking spray; set aside.

2. Combine whole wheat flour, all-purpose flour, 2 tablespoons wheat germ, baking powder, chives and sugar in medium bowl. Cut in margarine with pastry blender or two knives until mixture resembles coarse meal. Add milk and American cheese; stir until just combined.

3. Drop dough by rounded teaspoonfuls about 1 inch apart onto prepared baking sheet. Sprinkle with remaining 1 tablespoon wheat germ. Bake 10 to 12 minutes or until golden brown. Remove immediately from baking sheet. Serve warm.   *Makes 12 servings*

Chive Whole Wheat Drop Biscuits

PARMESAN GARLIC TWISTS

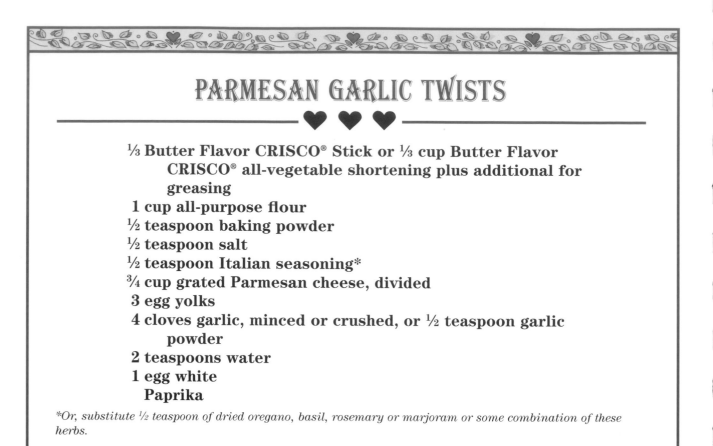

♥ ♥ ♥

⅓ Butter Flavor CRISCO® Stick or ⅓ cup Butter Flavor
    CRISCO® all-vegetable shortening plus additional for
    greasing
1 cup all-purpose flour
½ teaspoon baking powder
½ teaspoon salt
½ teaspoon Italian seasoning*
¾ cup grated Parmesan cheese, divided
3 egg yolks
4 cloves garlic, minced or crushed, or ½ teaspoon garlic
    powder
2 teaspoons water
1 egg white
    Paprika

Or, substitute ½ teaspoon of dried oregano, basil, rosemary or marjoram or some combination of these herbs.

1. Heat oven to 400°F. Grease baking sheets with shortening. Place sheets of foil on countertop for cooling garlic twists.

2. Combine flour, baking powder, salt and Italian seasoning in large bowl. Reserve 1 tablespoon Parmesan cheese. Add remaining cheese to flour mixture. Cut in ⅓ cup shortening with pastry blender (or two knives) until mixture resembles coarse crumbs. Beat egg yolks, garlic and water lightly. Sprinkle over flour mixture. Toss lightly with fork until dough forms ball. Flour lightly.

3. Roll dough out on floured surface or between two sheets of waxed paper to form 13×9-inch rectangle. Trim edges to straighten.

4. Cut in half crosswise. Cut strips ¼ inch wide (they will be 6½ inches long). Twist two strips together, overlapping each strip over the other. Place 2 inches apart on prepared baking sheets. Repeat until all strips are twists. Brush with egg white. Sprinkle with reserved Parmesan cheese.

5. Bake at 400°F for 8 to 10 minutes or until lightly browned. *Do not overbake.* Cool 1 minute. Remove to foil to cool completely. Sprinkle with paprika.

Makes 3 dozen twists

Parmesan Garlic Twists

TOMATO CHEESE BREAD

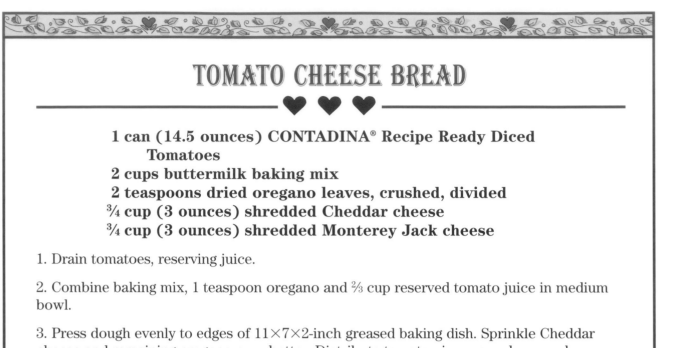

1 can (14.5 ounces) CONTADINA® Recipe Ready Diced
Tomatoes
2 cups buttermilk baking mix
2 teaspoons dried oregano leaves, crushed, divided
¾ cup (3 ounces) shredded Cheddar cheese
¾ cup (3 ounces) shredded Monterey Jack cheese

1. Drain tomatoes, reserving juice.

2. Combine baking mix, 1 teaspoon oregano and ⅔ cup reserved tomato juice in medium bowl.

3. Press dough evenly to edges of 11×7×2-inch greased baking dish. Sprinkle Cheddar cheese and remaining oregano over batter. Distribute tomato pieces evenly over cheese; sprinkle with Jack cheese.

4. Bake in preheated 375°F oven 25 minutes, or until edges are golden brown and cheese is bubbly. Cool 5 minutes before cutting into squares to serve.   *Makes 12 servings*

BASIL BISCUITS

2 cups all-purpose flour
4 tablespoons grated Parmesan cheese, divided
1 tablespoon baking powder
½ teaspoon baking soda
¼ teaspoon salt (optional)
4 tablespoons Neufchâtel cheese
2 tablespoons margarine, divided
6 ounces plain nonfat yogurt
⅓ cup slivered fresh basil leaves

1. Combine flour, 2 tablespoons Parmesan, baking powder, baking soda and salt in large bowl. Cut in Neufchâtel and 1 tablespoon margarine with pastry blender or two knives until mixture forms coarse crumbs. Stir in yogurt and basil, mixing just until dough clings together. Turn dough out onto lightly floured surface and gently pat into ball. Knead just until dough holds together. Pat and roll dough into 7-inch log. Cut into 7 (1-inch-thick) slices.

2. Spray 10-inch cast iron skillet or Dutch oven with nonstick cooking spray; arrange biscuits in skillet. Melt remaining 1 tablespoon margarine and brush over biscuit tops. Sprinkle with remaining 2 tablespoons Parmesan. Place skillet on grid set 4 to 6 inches above medium-hot coals (about 375°F); cover grill. Bake 20 to 40 minutes or until golden and firm on top.

Makes 7 biscuits

Note: To prepare a charcoal grill for baking, arrange a single, solid, even layer of medium coals in bottom of charcoal grill. If necessary, reduce temperature by either allowing coals to cook down or removing 3 or 4 coals at a time to a fireproof container until desired temperature is reached. For a gas grill, begin on medium heat and adjust heat as necessary. Besides raising or lowering the temperature setting, you can turn off one side of the grill or set each side to a different temperature.

DILLY CHEESE MUFFINS
♥ ♥ ♥

> 2 cups all-purpose flour
> 1 tablespoon sugar
> 1 tablespoon baking powder
> 2 teaspoons dried dill weed
> 1 teaspoon onion powder
> ½ teaspoon salt
> ¼ teaspoon black pepper
> 1 cup creamed small curd cottage cheese
> ¾ cup milk
> ¼ cup margarine or butter, melted
> 1 egg, beaten

Preheat oven to 400°F. Grease or paper-line 12 (2½-inch) muffin cups. Combine flour, sugar, baking powder, dill weed, onion powder, salt and pepper in large bowl. Combine cottage cheese, milk, margarine and egg in small bowl until blended; stir into flour mixture just until moistened. Spoon into muffin cups. Bake 20 to 25 minutes or until golden and toothpicks inserted into centers come out clean. Remove from pan.

Makes 12 muffins

BACON-CHEESE MUFFINS

♥ ♥ ♥

½ pound bacon (10 to 12 slices)
Vegetable oil
1 egg, beaten
¾ cup milk
1¾ cups all-purpose flour
¼ cup sugar
1 tablespoon baking powder
1 cup (4 ounces) shredded Wisconsin Cheddar cheese
½ cup crunchy nutlike cereal nuggets

Preheat oven to 400°F. In large skillet, cook bacon over medium-high heat until crisp. Drain, reserving drippings. If necessary, add oil to drippings to measure ⅓ cup. In small bowl, combine dripping mixture, egg and milk; set aside. Crumble bacon; set aside.

In large bowl, combine flour, sugar and baking powder. Make well in center. Add egg mixture all at once to flour mixture, stirring just until moistened. Batter should be lumpy. Fold in bacon, cheese and cereal. Spoon into greased or paper-lined 2½-inch muffin cups, filling about ¾ full. Bake 15 to 20 minutes or until golden. Remove from pan. Cool on wire rack. *Makes 12 muffins*

Favorite recipe from **Wisconsin Milk Marketing Board**

QUICK CORN BREAD WITH CHILIES 'N' CHEESE

♥ ♥ ♥

1 package (12 to 16 ounces) corn bread or corn muffin mix
1 cup (4 ounces) shredded Monterey Jack cheese, divided
1 can (4 ounces) chopped green chilies, drained
1 envelope LIPTON® RECIPE SECRETS® Vegetable Soup Mix

Prepare corn bread mix according to package directions; stir in ½ cup cheese, chilies and vegetable soup mix. Pour batter into lightly greased 8-inch baking pan; bake as directed. While warm, top with remaining ½ cup cheese. Cool completely on wire rack. To serve, cut into squares. *Makes 16 servings*

Bacon-Cheese Muffins

ACKNOWLEDGMENTS

The publisher would like to thank the companies and organizations listed below for the use of their recipes and photographs in this publication.

Arm & Hammer Division, Church & Dwight Co., Inc.

Birds Eye®

Bob Evans®

California Strawberry Commission

Cherry Marketing Institute

ConAgra Foods®

Del Monte Corporation

Dole Food Company, Inc.

Domino® Foods, Inc.

Duncan Hines® and Moist Deluxe® are registered trademarks of Aurora Foods Inc.

Eagle Brand®

Equal® sweetener

Fleischmann's® Yeast

Grandma's® is a registered trademark of Mott's, Inc.

Hershey Foods Corporation

Keebler® Company

© Mars, Incorporated 2004

McIlhenny Company (TABASCO® brand Pepper Sauce)

Mott's® is a registered trademark of Mott's, Inc.

National Honey Board

Nestlé USA

Newman's Own, Inc.®

The Quaker® Oatmeal Kitchens

Reckitt Benckiser Inc.

The J.M. Smucker Company

The Sugar Association, Inc.

Reprinted with permission of Sunkist Growers, Inc.

Texas Peanut Producers Board

Unilever Bestfoods North America

Walnut Marketing Board

Washington Apple Commission

Wisconsin Milk Marketing Board

INDEX